Improving Performance
Complete Self-Assessment Guide

C000157599

The guidance in this Self-Assessment is based ⟨
best practices and standards in business process architecture, design
and quality management. The guidance is also based on the professional
judgment of the individual collaborators listed in the Acknowledgments.

Notice of rights

The information in this book is distributed on an "As Is" basis without
warranty. While every precaution has been taken in the preparation of he
book, neither the author nor the publisher shall have any liability to any
person or entity with respect to any loss or damage caused or alleged to
be caused directly or indirectly by the instructions contained in this book
or by the products described in it.

Trademarks

Many of the designations used by manufacturers and sellers to
distinguish their products are claimed as trademarks. Where those
designations appear in this book, and the publisher was aware of a
trademark claim, the designations appear as requested by the owner
of the trademark. All other product names and services identified
throughout this book are used in editorial fashion only and for the
benefit of such companies with no intention of infringement of the
trademark. No such use, or the use of any trade name, is intended to
convey endorsement or other affiliation with this book.

Table of Contents

About The Art of Service

The Art of Service, Business Process Architects since 2000, is dedicated to helping stakeholders achieve excellence.

Defining, designing, creating, and implementing a process to solve a stakeholders challenge or meet an objective is the most valuable role… In EVERY group, company, organization and department.

Unless you're talking a one-time, single-use project, there should be a process. Whether that process is managed and implemented by humans, AI, or a combination of the two, it needs to be designed by someone with a complex enough perspective to ask the right questions.

Someone capable of asking the right questions and step back and say, 'What are we really trying to accomplish here? And is there a different way to look at it?'

With The Art of Service's Standard Requirements Self-Assessments, we empower people who can do just that — whether their title is marketer, entrepreneur, manager, salesperson, consultant, Business Process Manager, executive assistant, IT Manager, CIO etc... —they are the people who rule the future. They are people who watch the process as it happens, and ask the right questions to make the process work better.

Contact us when you need any support with this Self-Assessment and any help with templates, blue-prints and examples of standard documents you might need:

http://theartofservice.com
service@theartofservice.com

Acknowledgments

This checklist was developed under the auspices of The Art of Service, chaired by Gerardus Blokdyk.

Representatives from several client companies participated in the preparation of this Self-Assessment.

In addition, we are thankful for the design and printing services provided.

Included Resources - how to access

Included with your purchase of the book is the Improving Performance Self-Assessment Spreadsheet Dashboard which contains all questions and Self-Assessment areas and auto-generates insights, graphs, and project RACI planning - all with examples to get you started right away.

How? Simply send an email to
access@theartofservice.com
with this books' title in the subject to get the Improving Performance Self Assessment Tool right away.

You will receive the following contents with New and Updated specific criteria:

• The latest quick edition of the book in PDF

• The latest complete edition of the book in PDF, which criteria correspond to the criteria in...

• The Self-Assessment Excel Dashboard, and...

• Example pre-filled Self-Assessment Excel Dashboard to get familiar with results generation

• In-depth specific Checklists covering the topic

• Project management checklists and templates to assist with implementation

INCLUDES LIFETIME SELF ASSESSMENT UPDATES

Every self assessment comes with Lifetime Updates and Lifetime Free Updated Books. Lifetime Updates is an industry-first feature which allows you to receive verified self assessment updates, ensuring you always have the most accurate information at your fingertips.

Get it now- you will be glad you did - do it now, before you forget.

Send an email to **access@theartofservice.com** with this books' title in the subject to get the Improving Performance Self Assessment Tool right away.

Your feedback is invaluable to us

If you recently bought this book, we would love to hear from you! You can do this by writing a review on amazon (or the online store where you purchased this book) about your last purchase! As part of our continual service improvement process, we love to hear real client experiences and feedback.

How does it work?
To post a review on Amazon, just log in to your account and click on the Create Your Own Review button (under Customer Reviews) of the relevant product page. You can find examples of product reviews in Amazon. If you purchased from another online store, simply follow their procedures.

What happens when I submit my review?
Once you have submitted your review, send us an email at review@theartofservice.com with the link to your review so we can properly thank you for your feedback.

Purpose of this Self-Assessment

This Self-Assessment has been developed to improve understanding of the requirements and elements of Improving Performance, based on best practices and standards in business process architecture, design and quality management.

It is designed to allow for a rapid Self-Assessment to determine how closely existing management practices and procedures correspond to the elements of the Self-Assessment.

The criteria of requirements and elements of Improving Performance have been rephrased in the format of a Self-Assessment questionnaire, with a seven-criterion scoring system, as explained in this document.

In this format, even with limited background knowledge of

Improving Performance, a manager can quickly review existing operations to determine how they measure up to the standards. This in turn can serve as the starting point of a 'gap analysis' to identify management tools or system elements that might usefully be implemented in the organization to help improve overall performance.

How to use the Self-Assessment

On the following pages are a series of questions to identify to what extent your Improving Performance initiative is complete in comparison to the requirements set in standards.

To facilitate answering the questions, there is a space in front of each question to enter a score on a scale of '1' to '5'.

1 Strongly Disagree

2 Disagree

3 Neutral

4 Agree

5 Strongly Agree

Read the question and rate it with the following in front of mind:

'In my belief,
the answer to this question is clearly defined'.

There are two ways in which you can choose to interpret this statement;
1.   how aware are you that the answer to the question is clearly defined
2.   for more in-depth analysis you can choose to gather

evidence and confirm the answer to the question. This obviously will take more time, most Self-Assessment users opt for the first way to interpret the question and dig deeper later on based on the outcome of the overall Self-Assessment.

A score of '1' would mean that the answer is not clear at all, where a '5' would mean the answer is crystal clear and defined. Leave emtpy when the question is not applicable or you don't want to answer it, you can skip it without affecting your score. Write your score in the space provided.

After you have responded to all the appropriate statements in each section, compute your average score for that section, using the formula provided, and round to the nearest tenth. Then transfer to the corresponding spoke in the Improving Performance Scorecard on the second next page of the Self-Assessment.

Your completed Improving Performance Scorecard will give you a clear presentation of which Improving Performance areas need attention.

Improving Performance Scorecard Example

Example of how the finalized Scorecard can look like:

Improving Performance Scorecard

Your Scores:

BEGINNING OF THE SELF-ASSESSMENT:

CRITERION #1: RECOGNIZE

INTENT: Be aware of the need for change. Recognize that there is an unfavorable variation, problem or symptom.

In my belief, the answer to this question is clearly defined:

5 Strongly Agree

4 Agree

3 Neutral

2 Disagree

1 Strongly Disagree

1. How do you identify subcontractor relationships?
<--- Score

2. How do you recognize an improving performance objection?
<--- Score

3. Does the problem have ethical dimensions?
<--- Score

4. Will it solve real problems?
<--- Score

5. How do you recognize an objection?
<--- Score

6. Do you need to avoid or amend any improving performance activities?
<--- Score

7. What needs to stay?
<--- Score

8. What does improving performance success mean to the stakeholders?
<--- Score

9. What information do users need?
<--- Score

10. Do you recognize improving performance achievements?
<--- Score

11. Think about the people you identified for your improving performance project and the project responsibilities you would assign to them, what kind of training do you think they would need to perform these responsibilities effectively?
<--- Score

12. What situation(s) led to this improving performance Self Assessment?
<--- Score

13. What vendors make products that address the improving performance needs?
<--- Score

14. Are there any specific expectations or concerns about the improving performance team, improving performance itself?
<--- Score

15. Are you dealing with any of the same issues today as yesterday? What can you do about this?
<--- Score

16. How are you going to measure success?
<--- Score

17. What improving performance problem should be solved?
<--- Score

18. What creative shifts do you need to take?
<--- Score

19. Who are your key stakeholders who need to sign off?
<--- Score

20. How many trainings, in total, are needed?
<--- Score

21. Does improving performance create potential expectations in other areas that need to be recognized and considered?
<--- Score

22. Consider your own improving performance

project, what types of organizational problems do you think might be causing or affecting your problem, based on the work done so far?
<--- Score

23. What activities does the governance board need to consider?
<--- Score

24. Looking at each person individually – does every one have the qualities which are needed to work in this group?
<--- Score

25. How can auditing be a preventative security measure?
<--- Score

26. What are your needs in relation to improving performance skills, labor, equipment, and markets?
<--- Score

27. As a sponsor, customer or management, how important is it to meet goals, objectives?
<--- Score

28. Why the need?
<--- Score

29. Who else hopes to benefit from it?
<--- Score

30. Are there any revenue recognition issues?
<--- Score

31. Who defines the rules in relation to any given

issue?
<--- Score

32. What problems are you facing and how do you consider improving performance will circumvent those obstacles?
<--- Score

33. What are the improving performance resources needed?
<--- Score

34. Are controls defined to recognize and contain problems?
<--- Score

35. What is the improving performance problem definition? What do you need to resolve?
<--- Score

36. Do you need different information or graphics?
<--- Score

37. What is the problem or issue?
<--- Score

38. How are the improving performance's objectives aligned to the group's overall stakeholder strategy?
<--- Score

39. Is it needed?
<--- Score

40. Are there recognized improving performance problems?
<--- Score

41. How do you take a forward-looking perspective in identifying improving performance research related to market response and models?
<--- Score

42. Why is this needed?
<--- Score

43. Is it clear when you think of the day ahead of you what activities and tasks you need to complete?
<--- Score

44. Do you have/need 24-hour access to key personnel?
<--- Score

45. What extra resources will you need?
<--- Score

46. How are training requirements identified?
<--- Score

47. What prevents you from making the changes you know will make you a more effective improving performance leader?
<--- Score

48. What would happen if improving performance weren't done?
<--- Score

49. How does it fit into your organizational needs and tasks?
<--- Score

50. What resources or support might you need?
<--- Score

51. Can management personnel recognize the monetary benefit of improving performance?
<--- Score

52. Where do you need to exercise leadership?
<--- Score

53. Would you recognize a threat from the inside?
<--- Score

54. Who should resolve the improving performance issues?
<--- Score

55. What is the smallest subset of the problem you can usefully solve?
<--- Score

56. How much are sponsors, customers, partners, stakeholders involved in improving performance? In other words, what are the risks, if improving performance does not deliver successfully?
<--- Score

57. Will new equipment/products be required to facilitate improving performance delivery, for example is new software needed?
<--- Score

58. What tools and technologies are needed for a custom improving performance project?
<--- Score

59. What is the extent or complexity of the improving performance problem?
<--- Score

60. Will improving performance deliverables need to be tested and, if so, by whom?
<--- Score

61. Did you miss any major improving performance issues?
<--- Score

62. What are the minority interests and what amount of minority interests can be recognized?
<--- Score

63. Are losses recognized in a timely manner?
<--- Score

64. Who needs what information?
<--- Score

65. What else needs to be measured?
<--- Score

66. What improving performance events should you attend?
<--- Score

67. Are your goals realistic? Do you need to redefine your problem? Perhaps the problem has changed or maybe you have reached your goal and need to set a new one?
<--- Score

68. Which needs are not included or involved?

<--- Score

69. Who needs to know?
<--- Score

70. Who needs to know about improving performance?
<--- Score

71. Have you identified your improving performance key performance indicators?
<--- Score

72. What are the stakeholder objectives to be achieved with improving performance?
<--- Score

73. Are employees recognized or rewarded for performance that demonstrates the highest levels of integrity?
<--- Score

74. How do you assess your improving performance workforce capability and capacity needs, including skills, competencies, and staffing levels?
<--- Score

75. What are the clients issues and concerns?
<--- Score

76. What is the recognized need?
<--- Score

77. Which issues are too important to ignore?
<--- Score

78. Is the need for organizational change recognized?
<--- Score

79. When a improving performance manager recognizes a problem, what options are available?
<--- Score

80. Where is training needed?
<--- Score

81. What improving performance coordination do you need?
<--- Score

82. Are problem definition and motivation clearly presented?
<--- Score

83. What is the problem and/or vulnerability?
<--- Score

84. Whom do you really need or want to serve?
<--- Score

85. Do you know what you need to know about improving performance?
<--- Score

86. Are there improving performance problems defined?
<--- Score

87. Is the quality assurance team identified?
<--- Score

88. Are employees recognized for desired behaviors?

<--- Score

89. What training and capacity building actions are needed to implement proposed reforms?
<--- Score

90. What are the expected benefits of improving performance to the stakeholder?
<--- Score

91. What should be considered when identifying available resources, constraints, and deadlines?
<--- Score

92. What do employees need in the short term?
<--- Score

93. Which information does the improving performance business case need to include?
<--- Score

94. What improving performance capabilities do you need?
<--- Score

Add up total points for this section:
_ _ _ _ _ = Total points for this section

Divided by: _ _ _ _ _ _ (number of statements answered) = _ _ _ _ _ _ Average score for this section

Transfer your score to the improving performance Index at the beginning of the Self-Assessment.

CRITERION #2: DEFINE:

INTENT: Formulate the stakeholder problem. Define the problem, needs and objectives.

In my belief, the answer to this question is clearly defined:

5 Strongly Agree

4 Agree

3 Neutral

2 Disagree

1 Strongly Disagree

1. How will variation in the actual durations of each activity be dealt with to ensure that the expected improving performance results are met?
<--- Score

2. What is the scope of the improving performance work?
<--- Score

3. What defines best in class?
<--- Score

4. Does the scope remain the same?
<--- Score

5. What are the record-keeping requirements of improving performance activities?
<--- Score

6. Does the team have regular meetings?
<--- Score

7. What gets examined?
<--- Score

8. How do you keep key subject matter experts in the loop?
<--- Score

9. How would you define the culture at your organization, how susceptible is it to improving performance changes?
<--- Score

10. How do you hand over improving performance context?
<--- Score

11. Is there a critical path to deliver improving performance results?
<--- Score

12. Will team members regularly document their improving performance work?
<--- Score

13. What are the tasks and definitions?
<--- Score

14. What is the worst case scenario?
<--- Score

15. What sort of initial information to gather?
<--- Score

16. Has the improvement team collected the 'voice of the customer' (obtained feedback – qualitative and quantitative)?
<--- Score

17. Has the improving performance work been fairly and/or equitably divided and delegated among team members who are qualified and capable to perform the work? Has everyone contributed?
<--- Score

18. How did the improving performance manager receive input to the development of a improving performance improvement plan and the estimated completion dates/times of each activity?
<--- Score

19. How would you define improving performance leadership?
<--- Score

20. Are approval levels defined for contracts and supplements to contracts?
<--- Score

21. What baselines are required to be defined and

managed?
<--- Score

22. Is scope creep really all bad news?
<--- Score

23. Have specific policy objectives been defined?
<--- Score

24. What is the scope of improving performance?
<--- Score

25. What are the core elements of the improving
performance business case?
<--- Score

26. Has/have the customer(s) been identified?
<--- Score

27. Is the work to date meeting requirements?
<--- Score

28. How do you manage scope?
<--- Score

29. What are the boundaries of the scope? What is in
bounds and what is not? What is the start point? What
is the stop point?
<--- Score

30. Are different versions of process maps needed to
account for the different types of inputs?
<--- Score

31. What information should you gather?
<--- Score

32. Are roles and responsibilities formally defined?
<--- Score

33. Is there a improving performance management charter, including stakeholder case, problem and goal statements, scope, milestones, roles and responsibilities, communication plan?
<--- Score

34. Have all basic functions of improving performance been defined?
<--- Score

35. How do you gather the stories?
<--- Score

36. The political context: who holds power?
<--- Score

37. Do you have organizational privacy requirements?
<--- Score

38. What sources do you use to gather information for a improving performance study?
<--- Score

39. Is the improvement team aware of the different versions of a process: what they think it is vs. what it actually is vs. what it should be vs. what it could be?
<--- Score

40. What specifically is the problem? Where does it occur? When does it occur? What is its extent?
<--- Score

41. What are the dynamics of the communication plan?
<--- Score

42. Do the problem and goal statements meet the SMART criteria (specific, measurable, attainable, relevant, and time-bound)?
<--- Score

43. Why are you doing improving performance and what is the scope?
<--- Score

44. Do you have a improving performance success story or case study ready to tell and share?
<--- Score

45. How will the improving performance team and the group measure complete success of improving performance?
<--- Score

46. How have you defined all improving performance requirements first?
<--- Score

47. Is there a completed, verified, and validated high-level 'as is' (not 'should be' or 'could be') stakeholder process map?
<--- Score

48. Is there a completed SIPOC representation, describing the Suppliers, Inputs, Process, Outputs, and Customers?
<--- Score

49. Are improvement team members fully trained on improving performance?
<--- Score

50. When is the estimated completion date?
<--- Score

51. Has anyone else (internal or external to the group) attempted to solve this problem or a similar one before? If so, what knowledge can be leveraged from these previous efforts?
<--- Score

52. How do you gather requirements?
<--- Score

53. Have the customer needs been translated into specific, measurable requirements? How?
<--- Score

54. How is the team tracking and documenting its work?
<--- Score

55. Who are the improving performance improvement team members, including Management Leads and Coaches?
<--- Score

56. Has everyone on the team, including the team leaders, been properly trained?
<--- Score

57. What improving performance services do you require?
<--- Score

58. Is full participation by members in regularly held team meetings guaranteed?
<--- Score

59. Are audit criteria, scope, frequency and methods defined?
<--- Score

60. Has a high-level 'as is' process map been completed, verified and validated?
<--- Score

61. What are (control) requirements for improving performance Information?
<--- Score

62. What is out of scope?
<--- Score

63. Is the current 'as is' process being followed? If not, what are the discrepancies?
<--- Score

64. What are the improving performance use cases?
<--- Score

65. Is special improving performance user knowledge required?
<--- Score

66. How do you build the right business case?
<--- Score

67. What is the scope of the improving performance effort?

<--- Score

68. Are the improving performance requirements complete?
<--- Score

69. What is a worst-case scenario for losses?
<--- Score

70. Is data collected and displayed to better understand customer(s) critical needs and requirements.
<--- Score

71. Has a project plan, Gantt chart, or similar been developed/completed?
<--- Score

72. Is the team equipped with available and reliable resources?
<--- Score

73. How do you manage unclear improving performance requirements?
<--- Score

74. How was the 'as is' process map developed, reviewed, verified and validated?
<--- Score

75. What are the rough order estimates on cost savings/opportunities that improving performance brings?
<--- Score

76. How do you gather improving performance

requirements?
<--- Score

77. Are there different segments of customers?
<--- Score

78. What are the requirements for audit information?
<--- Score

79. Is it clearly defined in and to your organization what you do?
<--- Score

80. Who is gathering improving performance information?
<--- Score

81. Is improving performance required?
<--- Score

82. Are there any constraints known that bear on the ability to perform improving performance work? How is the team addressing them?
<--- Score

83. How does the improving performance manager ensure against scope creep?
<--- Score

84. What scope to assess?
<--- Score

85. Is the improving performance scope complete and appropriately sized?
<--- Score

86. Do you all define improving performance in the same way?
<--- Score

87. Who defines (or who defined) the rules and roles?
<--- Score

88. What are the compelling stakeholder reasons for embarking on improving performance?
<--- Score

89. Is there regularly 100% attendance at the team meetings? If not, have appointed substitutes attended to preserve cross-functionality and full representation?
<--- Score

90. Is the improving performance scope manageable?
<--- Score

91. Is improving performance currently on schedule according to the plan?
<--- Score

92. What is in scope?
<--- Score

93. What information do you gather?
<--- Score

94. Is there a clear improving performance case definition?
<--- Score

95. When are meeting minutes sent out? Who is on the distribution list?

<--- Score

96. What critical content must be communicated –
who, what, when, where, and how?
<--- Score

97. What knowledge or experience is required?
<--- Score

98. Are accountability and ownership for improving
performance clearly defined?
<--- Score

99. What is the definition of success?
<--- Score

100. What are the Roles and Responsibilities for
each team member and its leadership? Where is this
documented?
<--- Score

101. Will team members perform improving
performance work when assigned and in a timely
fashion?
<--- Score

102. Who is gathering information?
<--- Score

103. Has your scope been defined?
<--- Score

104. What is out-of-scope initially?
<--- Score

105. When is/was the improving performance start

date?
<--- Score

106. What constraints exist that might impact the team?
<--- Score

107. What intelligence can you gather?
<--- Score

108. What is in the scope and what is not in scope?
<--- Score

109. What customer feedback methods were used to solicit their input?
<--- Score

110. What key stakeholder process output measure(s) does improving performance leverage and how?
<--- Score

111. Has a team charter been developed and communicated?
<--- Score

112. Are required metrics defined, what are they?
<--- Score

113. If substitutes have been appointed, have they been briefed on the improving performance goals and received regular communications as to the progress to date?
<--- Score

114. Has the direction changed at all during the course of improving performance? If so, when did it

change and why?

<--- Score

115. How are consistent improving performance definitions important?

<--- Score

116. What improving performance requirements should be gathered?

<--- Score

117. Where can you gather more information?

<--- Score

118. How do you think the partners involved in improving performance would have defined success?

<--- Score

119. In what way can you redefine the criteria of choice clients have in your category in your favor?

<--- Score

120. Has a improving performance requirement not been met?

<--- Score

121. What is the definition of improving performance excellence?

<--- Score

122. What scope do you want your strategy to cover?

<--- Score

123. Scope of sensitive information?

<--- Score

124. Are customer(s) identified and segmented according to their different needs and requirements?
<--- Score

125. Are resources adequate for the scope?
<--- Score

126. What would be the goal or target for a improving performance's improvement team?
<--- Score

127. How do you catch improving performance definition inconsistencies?
<--- Score

128. Is there any additional improving performance definition of success?
<--- Score

129. Have all of the relationships been defined properly?
<--- Score

130. Is improving performance linked to key stakeholder goals and objectives?
<--- Score

131. How and when will the baselines be defined?
<--- Score

132. Are task requirements clearly defined?
<--- Score

133. How often are the team meetings?
<--- Score

134. Is the team adequately staffed with the desired cross-functionality? If not, what additional resources are available to the team?
<--- Score

Add up total points for this section:
_ _ _ _ _ = Total points for this section

Divided by: _ _ _ _ _ _ (number of statements answered) = _ _ _ _ _ _
Average score for this section

Transfer your score to the improving performance Index at the beginning of the Self-Assessment.

CRITERION #3: MEASURE:

INTENT: Gather the correct data. Measure the current performance and evolution of the situation.

In my belief, the answer to this question is clearly defined:

5 Strongly Agree

4 Agree

3 Neutral

2 Disagree

1 Strongly Disagree

1. What are the improving performance investment costs?
<--- Score

2. How much does it cost?
<--- Score

3. How do your measurements capture actionable improving performance information for use in

exceeding your customers expectations and securing your customers engagement?
<--- Score

4. What are your operating costs?
<--- Score

5. How are measurements made?
<--- Score

6. What are allowable costs?
<--- Score

7. What tests verify requirements?
<--- Score

8. At what cost?
<--- Score

9. How will measures be used to manage and adapt?
<--- Score

10. How do you measure success?
<--- Score

11. Why do the measurements/indicators matter?
<--- Score

12. What can be used to verify compliance?
<--- Score

13. What are your customers expectations and measures?
<--- Score

14. Which improving performance impacts are

significant?
<--- Score

15. What could cause delays in the schedule?
<--- Score

16. What evidence is there and what is measured?
<--- Score

17. How do you control the overall costs of your work processes?
<--- Score

18. Where can you go to verify the info?
<--- Score

19. What are the types and number of measures to use?
<--- Score

20. What details are required of the improving performance cost structure?
<--- Score

21. Are you able to realize any cost savings?
<--- Score

22. What are your primary costs, revenues, assets?
<--- Score

23. Are the measurements objective?
<--- Score

24. What causes innovation to fail or succeed in your organization?
<--- Score

25. How do you verify and develop ideas and innovations?
<--- Score

26. What causes extra work or rework?
<--- Score

27. What measurements are possible, practicable and meaningful?
<--- Score

28. What causes mismanagement?
<--- Score

29. Do the benefits outweigh the costs?
<--- Score

30. How is performance measured?
<--- Score

31. What is your decision requirements diagram?
<--- Score

32. How can a improving performance test verify your ideas or assumptions?
<--- Score

33. What are you verifying?
<--- Score

34. Are supply costs steady or fluctuating?
<--- Score

35. When should you bother with diagrams?
<--- Score

36. Are you aware of what could cause a problem?
<--- Score

37. How to cause the change?
<--- Score

38. How do you verify the improving performance requirements quality?
<--- Score

39. What methods are feasible and acceptable to estimate the impact of reforms?
<--- Score

40. What could cause you to change course?
<--- Score

41. What causes investor action?
<--- Score

42. Are there competing improving performance priorities?
<--- Score

43. How do you measure variability?
<--- Score

44. Is there an opportunity to verify requirements?
<--- Score

45. How do you verify and validate the improving performance data?
<--- Score

46. How will effects be measured?

<--- Score

47. Are the units of measure consistent?
<--- Score

48. Was a business case (cost/benefit) developed?
<--- Score

49. What would be a real cause for concern?
<--- Score

50. Do you have an issue in getting priority?
<--- Score

51. What is measured? Why?
<--- Score

52. What do you measure and why?
<--- Score

53. What is the cost of rework?
<--- Score

54. Does management have the right priorities among projects?
<--- Score

55. Are indirect costs charged to the improving performance program?
<--- Score

56. What is the root cause(s) of the problem?
<--- Score

57. How do you measure lifecycle phases?
<--- Score

58. How do you aggregate measures across priorities?
<--- Score

59. Which costs should be taken into account?
<--- Score

60. What is the total fixed cost?
<--- Score

61. When a disaster occurs, who gets priority?
<--- Score

62. Does a improving performance quantification method exist?
<--- Score

63. How will success or failure be measured?
<--- Score

64. Are you taking your company in the direction of better and revenue or cheaper and cost?
<--- Score

65. How is progress measured?
<--- Score

66. What are the costs of delaying improving performance action?
<--- Score

67. What harm might be caused?
<--- Score

68. Has a cost center been established?
<--- Score

69. What drives O&M cost?

<--- Score

70. What are the current costs of the improving performance process?

<--- Score

71. How will you measure your improving performance effectiveness?

<--- Score

72. Have you made assumptions about the shape of the future, particularly its impact on your customers and competitors?

<--- Score

73. Are actual costs in line with budgeted costs?

<--- Score

74. How do you verify performance?

<--- Score

75. Do you aggressively reward and promote the people who have the biggest impact on creating excellent improving performance services/products?

<--- Score

76. What are the costs?

<--- Score

77. What disadvantage does this cause for the user?

<--- Score

78. What is the cause of any improving performance gaps?

<--- Score

79. What does your operating model cost?
<--- Score

80. Are the improving performance benefits worth its costs?
<--- Score

81. Is the solution cost-effective?
<--- Score

82. What are your key improving performance organizational performance measures, including key short and longer-term financial measures?
<--- Score

83. How are costs allocated?
<--- Score

84. How will costs be allocated?
<--- Score

85. Who pays the cost?
<--- Score

86. How will your organization measure success?
<--- Score

87. Will improving performance have an impact on current business continuity, disaster recovery processes and/or infrastructure?
<--- Score

88. How long to keep data and how to manage retention costs?

<--- Score

89. What would it cost to replace your technology?
<--- Score

90. What relevant entities could be measured?
<--- Score

91. What is an unallowable cost?
<--- Score

92. What is your improving performance quality cost segregation study?
<--- Score

93. Do you have any cost improving performance limitation requirements?
<--- Score

94. What are hidden improving performance quality costs?
<--- Score

95. What do people want to verify?
<--- Score

96. What are the costs and benefits?
<--- Score

97. Have you included everything in your improving performance cost models?
<--- Score

98. What potential environmental factors impact the improving performance effort?
<--- Score

99. How will you measure success?
<--- Score

100. How can you measure improving performance in a systematic way?
<--- Score

101. What are the strategic priorities for this year?
<--- Score

102. How can you reduce costs?
<--- Score

103. Does rpa drive down costs while improving performance and efficiency in your organization, how do yo know, what are your measurements?
<--- Score

104. What is the improving performance business impact?
<--- Score

105. What are the estimated costs of proposed changes?
<--- Score

106. Where is the cost?
<--- Score

107. Are improving performance vulnerabilities categorized and prioritized?
<--- Score

108. How do you measure efficient delivery of improving performance services?

<--- Score

109. How do you prevent mis-estimating cost?
<--- Score

110. Have design-to-cost goals been established?
<--- Score

111. How can you manage cost down?
<--- Score

112. What are the operational costs after improving performance deployment?
<--- Score

113. When are costs are incurred?
<--- Score

114. How is the value delivered by improving performance being measured?
<--- Score

115. What are the improving performance key cost drivers?
<--- Score

116. How can you measure the performance?
<--- Score

117. How do you verify your resources?
<--- Score

118. What happens if cost savings do not materialize?
<--- Score

119. Does the improving performance task fit the

client's priorities?

<--- Score

120. How do you verify if improving performance is built right?

<--- Score

121. Among the improving performance product and service cost to be estimated, which is considered hardest to estimate?

<--- Score

122. Where is it measured?

<--- Score

123. What is the total cost related to deploying improving performance, including any consulting or professional services?

<--- Score

124. Are there any easy-to-implement alternatives to improving performance? Sometimes other solutions are available that do not require the cost implications of a full-blown project?

<--- Score

125. Do you effectively measure and reward individual and team performance?

<--- Score

126. Are missed improving performance opportunities costing your organization money?

<--- Score

127. What does verifying compliance entail?

<--- Score

128. Do you have a flow diagram of what happens?
<--- Score

129. Are there measurements based on task performance?
<--- Score

130. Why do you expend time and effort to implement measurement, for whom?
<--- Score

131. Do you verify that corrective actions were taken?
<--- Score

132. What does a Test Case verify?
<--- Score

133. What does losing customers cost your organization?
<--- Score

134. What measurements are being captured?
<--- Score

135. What users will be impacted?
<--- Score

136. Is it possible to estimate the impact of unanticipated complexity such as wrong or failed assumptions, feedback, etcetera on proposed reforms?
<--- Score

137. How can you reduce the costs of obtaining inputs?

<--- Score

138. How do you quantify and qualify impacts?
<--- Score

Add up total points for this section:
_____ = Total points for this section

Divided by: _____ (number of
statements answered) = _____
Average score for this section

Transfer your score to the improving
performance Index at the beginning of
the Self-Assessment.

CRITERION #4: ANALYZE:

INTENT: Analyze causes, assumptions and hypotheses.

In my belief, the answer to this question is clearly defined:

5 Strongly Agree

4 Agree

3 Neutral

2 Disagree

1 Strongly Disagree

1. What are the improving performance design outputs?
<--- Score

2. Who qualifies to gain access to data?
<--- Score

3. How do your work systems and key work processes relate to and capitalize on your core competencies?
<--- Score

4. Do you have the authority to produce the output?
<--- Score

5. How do you implement and manage your work processes to ensure that they meet design requirements?
<--- Score

6. What qualifications and skills do you need?
<--- Score

7. What successful thing are you doing today that may be blinding you to new growth opportunities?
<--- Score

8. How has the improving performance data been gathered?
<--- Score

9. What output to create?
<--- Score

10. What does the data say about the performance of the stakeholder process?
<--- Score

11. Do your leaders quickly bounce back from setbacks?
<--- Score

12. Are you missing improving performance opportunities?
<--- Score

13. What is the cost of poor quality as supported by

the team's analysis?
<--- Score

14. What conclusions were drawn from the team's data collection and analysis? How did the team reach these conclusions?
<--- Score

15. How much data can be collected in the given timeframe?
<--- Score

16. What qualifies as competition?
<--- Score

17. Were any designed experiments used to generate additional insight into the data analysis?
<--- Score

18. Is the improving performance process severely broken such that a re-design is necessary?
<--- Score

19. Have the problem and goal statements been updated to reflect the additional knowledge gained from the analyze phase?
<--- Score

20. What process should you select for improvement?
<--- Score

21. What tools were used to narrow the list of possible causes?
<--- Score

22. An organizationally feasible system request is one

that considers the mission, goals and objectives of the organization, key questions are: is the improving performance solution request practical and will it solve a problem or take advantage of an opportunity to achieve company goals?
<--- Score

23. Is there an established change management process?
<--- Score

24. Record-keeping requirements flow from the records needed as inputs, outputs, controls and for transformation of a improving performance process, are the records needed as inputs to the improving performance process available?
<--- Score

25. What improving performance data do you gather or use now?
<--- Score

26. What improving performance metrics are outputs of the process?
<--- Score

27. What, related to, improving performance processes does your organization outsource?
<--- Score

28. How do you measure the operational performance of your key work systems and processes, including productivity, cycle time, and other appropriate measures of process effectiveness, efficiency, and innovation?
<--- Score

29. How do you promote understanding that opportunity for improvement is not criticism of the status quo, or the people who created the status quo?
<--- Score

30. Was a cause-and-effect diagram used to explore the different types of causes (or sources of variation)?
<--- Score

31. Is the gap/opportunity displayed and communicated in financial terms?
<--- Score

32. What is the Value Stream Mapping?
<--- Score

33. Do your employees have the opportunity to do what they do best everyday?
<--- Score

34. What methods do you use to gather improving performance data?
<--- Score

35. What information qualified as important?
<--- Score

36. Are improving performance changes recognized early enough to be approved through the regular process?
<--- Score

37. What data is gathered?
<--- Score

38. Is the performance gap determined?
<--- Score

39. What do you need to qualify?
<--- Score

40. Do quality systems drive continuous improvement?
<--- Score

41. What resources go in to get the desired output?
<--- Score

42. What are your outputs?
<--- Score

43. What improving performance data should be collected?
<--- Score

44. What are your best practices for minimizing improving performance project risk, while demonstrating incremental value and quick wins throughout the improving performance project lifecycle?
<--- Score

45. How is data used for program management and improvement?
<--- Score

46. How is the way you as the leader think and process information affecting your organizational culture?
<--- Score

47. Do you, as a leader, bounce back quickly from

setbacks?
<--- Score

48. Where is the data coming from to measure compliance?
<--- Score

49. Who will facilitate the team and process?
<--- Score

50. Have any additional benefits been identified that will result from closing all or most of the gaps?
<--- Score

51. Are all staff in core improving performance subjects Highly Qualified?
<--- Score

52. What tools were used to generate the list of possible causes?
<--- Score

53. Have you defined which data is gathered how?
<--- Score

54. Where is improving performance data gathered?
<--- Score

55. What other jobs or tasks affect the performance of the steps in the improving performance process?
<--- Score

56. Did any additional data need to be collected?
<--- Score

57. Do your contracts/agreements contain data

security obligations?

<--- Score

58. What are the necessary qualifications?

<--- Score

59. When should a process be art not science?

<--- Score

60. What did the team gain from developing a sub-process map?

<--- Score

61. How will the improving performance data be captured?

<--- Score

62. How can risk management be tied procedurally to process elements?

<--- Score

63. What are your current levels and trends in key measures or indicators of improving performance product and process performance that are important to and directly serve your customers? How do these results compare with the performance of your competitors and other organizations with similar offerings?

<--- Score

64. Did any value-added analysis or 'lean thinking' take place to identify some of the gaps shown on the 'as is' process map?

<--- Score

65. What qualifications do improving performance

leaders need?

<--- Score

66. How many input/output points does it require?

<--- Score

67. What improving performance data will be collected?

<--- Score

68. Should you invest in industry-recognized qualifications?

<--- Score

69. How do you identify specific improving performance investment opportunities and emerging trends?

<--- Score

70. Who owns what data?

<--- Score

71. What controls do you have in place to protect data?

<--- Score

72. What are your current levels and trends in key improving performance measures or indicators of product and process performance that are important to and directly serve your customers?

<--- Score

73. Were there any improvement opportunities identified from the process analysis?

<--- Score

74. What are the best opportunities for value improvement?
<--- Score

75. What training and qualifications will you need?
<--- Score

76. How do you ensure that the improving performance opportunity is realistic?
<--- Score

77. Are your outputs consistent?
<--- Score

78. What were the financial benefits resulting from any 'ground fruit or low-hanging fruit' (quick fixes)?
<--- Score

79. How will the data be checked for quality?
<--- Score

80. What are your key performance measures or indicators and in-process measures for the control and improvement of your improving performance processes?
<--- Score

81. What is the output?
<--- Score

82. What systems/processes must you excel at?
<--- Score

83. Are all team members qualified for all tasks?
<--- Score

84. How is the data gathered?
<--- Score

85. Has an output goal been set?
<--- Score

86. How are outputs preserved and protected?
<--- Score

87. What data do you need to collect?
<--- Score

88. What is the complexity of the output produced?
<--- Score

89. How was the detailed process map generated,
verified, and validated?
<--- Score

90. What qualifications are necessary?
<--- Score

91. What are your improving performance processes?
<--- Score

92. How will the change process be managed?
<--- Score

93. Who is involved with workflow mapping?
<--- Score

94. Is data and process analysis, root cause analysis
and quantifying the gap/opportunity in place?
<--- Score

95. Should the data be in the cloud for improving

performance?
<--- Score

96. Has data output been validated?
<--- Score

97. How do you use improving performance data and information to support organizational decision making and innovation?
<--- Score

98. How will corresponding data be collected?
<--- Score

99. Were Pareto charts (or similar) used to portray the 'heavy hitters' (or key sources of variation)?
<--- Score

100. How does the organization define, manage, and improve its improving performance processes?
<--- Score

101. Think about some of the processes you undertake within your organization, which do you own?
<--- Score

102. Is the required improving performance data gathered?
<--- Score

103. What are evaluation criteria for the output?
<--- Score

104. What are the disruptive improving performance technologies that enable your organization to

radically change your business processes?
<--- Score

105. What internal processes need improvement?
<--- Score

106. Do you understand your management processes today?
<--- Score

107. What will drive improving performance change?
<--- Score

108. What process improvements will be needed?
<--- Score

109. Can you add value to the current improving performance decision-making process (largely qualitative) by incorporating uncertainty modeling (more quantitative)?
<--- Score

110. How do you define collaboration and team output?
<--- Score

111. Was a detailed process map created to amplify critical steps of the 'as is' stakeholder process?
<--- Score

112. Is the final output clearly identified?
<--- Score

113. What were the crucial 'moments of truth' on the process map?
<--- Score

114. How is the improving performance Value Stream Mapping managed?
<--- Score

115. Who is involved in the management review process?
<--- Score

116. What are the improving performance business drivers?
<--- Score

117. Who will gather what data?
<--- Score

118. Is the suppliers process defined and controlled?
<--- Score

119. What types of data do your improving performance indicators require?
<--- Score

120. What improving performance data should be managed?
<--- Score

121. Do staff qualifications match your project?
<--- Score

122. Is pre-qualification of suppliers carried out?
<--- Score

123. How is improving performance data gathered?
<--- Score

124. What are the processes for audit reporting and management?
<--- Score

125. What qualifications are needed?
<--- Score

126. What quality tools were used to get through the analyze phase?
<--- Score

127. What is the improving performance Driver?
<--- Score

128. What other organizational variables, such as reward systems or communication systems, affect the performance of this improving performance process?
<--- Score

129. Is there any way to speed up the process?
<--- Score

130. Identify an operational issue in your organization, for example, could a particular task be done more quickly or more efficiently by improving performance?
<--- Score

131. How do mission and objectives affect the improving performance processes of your organization?
<--- Score

132. Think about the functions involved in your improving performance project, what processes flow from these functions?

<--- Score

133. A compounding model resolution with available relevant data can often provide insight towards a solution methodology; which improving performance models, tools and techniques are necessary?
<--- Score

134. What are the personnel training and qualifications required?
<--- Score

135. What are the revised rough estimates of the financial savings/opportunity for improving performance improvements?
<--- Score

136. Are gaps between current performance and the goal performance identified?
<--- Score

137. What is the oversight process?
<--- Score

138. How often will data be collected for measures?
<--- Score

Add up total points for this section:
_ _ _ _ _ = Total points for this section

Divided by: _ _ _ _ _ _ (number of statements answered) = _ _ _ _ _ _
Average score for this section

Transfer your score to the improving performance Index at the beginning of

the Self-Assessment.

CRITERION #5: IMPROVE:

INTENT: Develop a practical solution.
Innovate, establish and test the
solution and to measure the results.

In my belief, the answer to this
question is clearly defined:

5 Strongly Agree

4 Agree

3 Neutral

2 Disagree

1 Strongly Disagree

1. How do you go about comparing improving
performance approaches/solutions?
<--- Score

2. Which of the recognised risks out of all risks can be
most likely transferred?
<--- Score

3. What were the criteria for evaluating a improving

performance pilot?
<--- Score

4. What criteria will you use to assess your improving performance risks?
<--- Score

5. Is any improving performance documentation required?
<--- Score

6. What tools do you use once you have decided on a improving performance strategy and more importantly how do you choose?
<--- Score

7. Who are the key stakeholders for the improving performance evaluation?
<--- Score

8. How will you know that a change is an improvement?
<--- Score

9. What area needs the greatest improvement?
<--- Score

10. How are improving performance risks managed?
<--- Score

11. When you map the key players in your own work and the types/domains of relationships with them, which relationships do you find easy and which challenging, and why?
<--- Score

12. How scalable is your improving performance solution?
<--- Score

13. What strategies for improving performance improvement are successful?
<--- Score

14. What are the implications of the one critical improving performance decision 10 minutes, 10 months, and 10 years from now?
<--- Score

15. How can skill-level changes improve improving performance?
<--- Score

16. What to do with the results or outcomes of measurements?
<--- Score

17. Do you need to do a usability evaluation?
<--- Score

18. How will you know when its improved?
<--- Score

19. How do you define the solutions' scope?
<--- Score

20. Is the measure of success for improving performance understandable to a variety of people?
<--- Score

21. How does your organization evaluate strategic improving performance success?

<--- Score

22. What alternative responses are available to manage risk?
<--- Score

23. Can the solution be designed and implemented within an acceptable time period?
<--- Score

24. What tools were used to evaluate the potential solutions?
<--- Score

25. Who will be using the results of the measurement activities?
<--- Score

26. improving performance risk decisions: whose call Is It?
<--- Score

27. Is supporting improving performance documentation required?
<--- Score

28. Who manages supplier risk management in your organization?
<--- Score

29. How do you measure risk?
<--- Score

30. How are policy decisions made and where?
<--- Score

31. What practices helps your organization to develop its capacity to recognize patterns?
<--- Score

32. What improving performance improvements can be made?
<--- Score

33. Who will be responsible for documenting the improving performance requirements in detail?
<--- Score

34. What can you do to improve?
<--- Score

35. Explorations of the frontiers of improving performance will help you build influence, improve improving performance, optimize decision making, and sustain change, what is your approach?
<--- Score

36. What are your current levels and trends in key measures or indicators of workforce and leader development?
<--- Score

37. What current systems have to be understood and/or changed?
<--- Score

38. What were the underlying assumptions on the cost-benefit analysis?
<--- Score

39. Will the controls trigger any other risks?
<--- Score

40. For decision problems, how do you develop a decision statement?
<--- Score

41. What are the expectations of your boss with respect to improving performance from one project to the next?
<--- Score

42. How will you know that you have improved?
<--- Score

43. How do you improve productivity?
<--- Score

44. Is the improving performance solution sustainable?
<--- Score

45. Do vendor agreements bring new compliance risk ?
<--- Score

46. Who controls key decisions that will be made?
<--- Score

47. Where do the improving performance decisions reside?
<--- Score

48. For estimation problems, how do you develop an estimation statement?
<--- Score

49. At what point will vulnerability assessments be

performed once improving performance is put into production (e.g., ongoing Risk Management after implementation)?
<--- Score

50. Do you have the optimal project management team structure?
<--- Score

51. Is the solution technically practical?
<--- Score

52. In the past few months, what is the smallest change you have made that has had the biggest positive result? What was it about that small change that produced the large return?
<--- Score

53. Is the scope clearly documented?
<--- Score

54. What needs improvement? Why?
<--- Score

55. How is knowledge sharing about risk management improved?
<--- Score

56. What tools were used to tap into the creativity and encourage 'outside the box' thinking?
<--- Score

57. How do you measure improved improving performance service perception, and satisfaction?
<--- Score

58. What are the improving performance security risks?

<--- Score

59. Who manages improving performance risk?

<--- Score

60. How do you manage improving performance risk?

<--- Score

61. Is the improving performance documentation thorough?

<--- Score

62. What is the magnitude of the improvements?

<--- Score

63. How do you deal with improving performance risk?

<--- Score

64. How can you better manage risk?

<--- Score

65. Risk events: what are the things that could go wrong?

<--- Score

66. Who controls the risk?

<--- Score

67. How do you decide how much to remunerate an employee?

<--- Score

68. Is there any other improving performance

solution?

<--- Score

69. Have you identified breakpoints and/or risk tolerances that will trigger broad consideration of a potential need for intervention or modification of strategy?

<--- Score

70. How risky is your organization?

<--- Score

71. What risks do you need to manage?

<--- Score

72. Are the key business and technology risks being managed?

<--- Score

73. How do you improve your likelihood of success ?

<--- Score

74. How do you link measurement and risk?

<--- Score

75. Are decisions made in a timely manner?

<--- Score

76. Was a improving performance charter developed?

<--- Score

77. Do you combine technical expertise with business knowledge and improving performance Key topics include lifecycles, development approaches, requirements and how to make a business case?

<--- Score

78. Why improve in the first place?
<--- Score

79. Are you assessing improving performance and risk?
<--- Score

80. Risk Identification: What are the possible risk events your organization faces in relation to improving performance?
<--- Score

81. What are the concrete improving performance results?
<--- Score

82. Is there a high likelihood that any recommendations will achieve their intended results?
<--- Score

83. How do the improving performance results compare with the performance of your competitors and other organizations with similar offerings?
<--- Score

84. How can an OEE solution assist operations management with improving performance in real time (on the production floor)?
<--- Score

85. Are the most efficient solutions problem-specific?
<--- Score

86. What is the improving performance's sustainability risk?

<--- Score

87. Do those selected for the improving performance team have a good general understanding of what improving performance is all about?
<--- Score

88. Are risk management tasks balanced centrally and locally?
<--- Score

89. Would you develop a improving performance Communication Strategy?
<--- Score

90. If you could go back in time five years, what decision would you make differently? What is your best guess as to what decision you're making today you might regret five years from now?
<--- Score

91. How can the phases of improving performance development be identified?
<--- Score

92. How is continuous improvement applied to risk management?
<--- Score

93. Is the improving performance risk managed?
<--- Score

94. Who makes the improving performance decisions in your organization?
<--- Score

95. What is improving performance risk?
<--- Score

96. What do you want to improve?
<--- Score

97. How can you improve performance?
<--- Score

98. Who will be responsible for making the decisions to include or exclude requested changes once improving performance is underway?
<--- Score

99. To what extent does management recognize improving performance as a tool to increase the results?
<--- Score

100. In what ways does the senior leadership team collectively contribute to improving performance?
<--- Score

101. Is improving performance documentation maintained?
<--- Score

102. What actually has to improve and by how much?
<--- Score

103. Who do you report improving performance results to?
<--- Score

104. Are procedures documented for managing improving performance risks?

<--- Score

105. Does the goal represent a desired result that can be measured?
<--- Score

106. Are events managed to resolution?
<--- Score

107. Risk factors: what are the characteristics of improving performance that make it risky?
<--- Score

108. Who should make the improving performance decisions?
<--- Score

109. How does the team improve its work?
<--- Score

110. Who are the people involved in developing and implementing improving performance?
<--- Score

111. What resources are required for the improvement efforts?
<--- Score

112. Are the risks fully understood, reasonable and manageable?
<--- Score

113. Who are the improving performance decision-makers?
<--- Score

114. What assumptions are made about the solution and approach?
<--- Score

115. How can you improve improving performance?
<--- Score

116. Can you integrate quality management and risk management?
<--- Score

117. How do you manage and improve your improving performance work systems to deliver customer value and achieve organizational success and sustainability?
<--- Score

118. How will you measure the results?
<--- Score

119. Do you cover the five essential competencies: Communication, Collaboration,Innovation, Adaptability, and Leadership that improve an organizations ability to leverage the new improving performance in a volatile global economy?
<--- Score

120. Can you identify any significant risks or exposures to improving performance third- parties (vendors, service providers, alliance partners etc) that concern you?
<--- Score

121. How significant is the improvement in the eyes of the end user?
<--- Score

122. How will you recognize and celebrate results?
<--- Score

123. What is the risk?
<--- Score

124. How do you improve improving performance service perception, and satisfaction?
<--- Score

125. Are risk triggers captured?
<--- Score

126. How do you measure progress and evaluate training effectiveness?
<--- Score

127. What improvements have been achieved?
<--- Score

128. How do you keep improving improving performance?
<--- Score

129. Is risk periodically assessed?
<--- Score

130. Which improving performance solution is appropriate?
<--- Score

131. Who are the improving performance decision makers?
<--- Score

Add up total points for this section:
_____ = Total points for this section

Divided by: _____ (number of
statements answered) = _____
Average score for this section

Transfer your score to the improving
performance Index at the beginning of
the Self-Assessment.

CRITERION #6: CONTROL:

INTENT: Implement the practical solution. Maintain the performance and correct possible complications.

In my belief, the answer to this question is clearly defined:

5 Strongly Agree

4 Agree

3 Neutral

2 Disagree

1 Strongly Disagree

1. Does the improving performance performance meet the customer's requirements?
<--- Score

2. Is there an action plan in case of emergencies?
<--- Score

3. Will any special training be provided for results interpretation?

<--- Score

4. Implementation Planning: is a pilot needed to test the changes before a full roll out occurs?
<--- Score

5. How do you monitor usage and cost?
<--- Score

6. How will report readings be checked to effectively monitor performance?
<--- Score

7. What is the control/monitoring plan?
<--- Score

8. Are you measuring, monitoring and predicting improving performance activities to optimize operations and profitability, and enhancing outcomes?
<--- Score

9. Who sets the improving performance standards?
<--- Score

10. Do the improving performance decisions you make today help people and the planet tomorrow?
<--- Score

11. You may have created your quality measures at a time when you lacked resources, technology wasn't up to the required standard, or low service levels were the industry norm. Have those circumstances changed?
<--- Score

12. Will existing staff require re-training, for example, to learn new business processes?
<--- Score

13. Are controls in place and consistently applied?
<--- Score

14. How is improving performance project cost planned, managed, monitored?
<--- Score

15. What are you attempting to measure/monitor?
<--- Score

16. What is your plan to assess your security risks?
<--- Score

17. How can you best use all of your knowledge repositories to enhance learning and sharing?
<--- Score

18. What is the recommended frequency of auditing?
<--- Score

19. What should the next improvement project be that is related to improving performance?
<--- Score

20. Is there a transfer of ownership and knowledge to process owner and process team tasked with the responsibilities.
<--- Score

21. What are the critical parameters to watch?
<--- Score

22. What other areas of the group might benefit from the improving performance team's improvements, knowledge, and learning?
<--- Score

23. How will new or emerging customer needs/requirements be checked/communicated to orient the process toward meeting the new specifications and continually reducing variation?
<--- Score

24. How is change control managed?
<--- Score

25. How do you plan for the cost of succession?
<--- Score

26. Are the planned controls in place?
<--- Score

27. Has the improved process and its steps been standardized?
<--- Score

28. Does a troubleshooting guide exist or is it needed?
<--- Score

29. What are the performance and scale of the improving performance tools?
<--- Score

30. What quality tools were useful in the control phase?
<--- Score

31. What are your results for key measures or

indicators of the accomplishment of your improving performance strategy and action plans, including building and strengthening core competencies?
<--- Score

32. Is there documentation that will support the successful operation of the improvement?
<--- Score

33. What other systems, operations, processes, and infrastructures (hiring practices, staffing, training, incentives/rewards, metrics/dashboards/scorecards, etc.) need updates, additions, changes, or deletions in order to facilitate knowledge transfer and improvements?
<--- Score

34. Who controls critical resources?
<--- Score

35. Who will be in control?
<--- Score

36. Where do ideas that reach policy makers and planners as proposals for improving performance strengthening and reform actually originate?
<--- Score

37. What can you control?
<--- Score

38. Who is going to spread your message?
<--- Score

39. How widespread is its use?
<--- Score

40. Are suggested corrective/restorative actions indicated on the response plan for known causes to problems that might surface?
<--- Score

41. Is reporting being used or needed?
<--- Score

42. Is there a improving performance Communication plan covering who needs to get what information when?
<--- Score

43. What do you stand for--and what are you against?
<--- Score

44. Is there a control plan in place for sustaining improvements (short and long-term)?
<--- Score

45. Are there documented procedures?
<--- Score

46. Does job training on the documented procedures need to be part of the process team's education and training?
<--- Score

47. Will your goals reflect your program budget?
<--- Score

48. How likely is the current improving performance plan to come in on schedule or on budget?
<--- Score

49. How will the process owner verify improvement in present and future sigma levels, process capabilities?
<--- Score

50. What are the known security controls?
<--- Score

51. Are new process steps, standards, and documentation ingrained into normal operations?
<--- Score

52. Does the response plan contain a definite closed loop continual improvement scheme (e.g., plan-do-check-act)?
<--- Score

53. Do you monitor the effectiveness of your improving performance activities?
<--- Score

54. How do you establish and deploy modified action plans if circumstances require a shift in plans and rapid execution of new plans?
<--- Score

55. How do you spread information?
<--- Score

56. How do your controls stack up?
<--- Score

57. How do you encourage people to take control and responsibility?
<--- Score

58. Can you adapt and adjust to changing improving

performance situations?
<--- Score

59. Are operating procedures consistent?
<--- Score

60. How do you plan on providing proper recognition and disclosure of supporting companies?
<--- Score

61. What are customers monitoring?
<--- Score

62. How do senior leaders actions reflect a commitment to the organizations improving performance values?
<--- Score

63. Does improving performance appropriately measure and monitor risk?
<--- Score

64. Will the team be available to assist members in planning investigations?
<--- Score

65. Is the improving performance test/monitoring cost justified?
<--- Score

66. Who has control over resources?
<--- Score

67. Do the viable solutions scale to future needs?
<--- Score

68. Is knowledge gained on process shared and institutionalized?
<--- Score

69. What is the standard for acceptable improving performance performance?
<--- Score

70. What do you measure to verify effectiveness gains?
<--- Score

71. Are pertinent alerts monitored, analyzed and distributed to appropriate personnel?
<--- Score

72. Are documented procedures clear and easy to follow for the operators?
<--- Score

73. Is a response plan in place for when the input, process, or output measures indicate an 'out-of-control' condition?
<--- Score

74. Is there a standardized process?
<--- Score

75. How will input, process, and output variables be checked to detect for sub-optimal conditions?
<--- Score

76. Is new knowledge gained imbedded in the response plan?
<--- Score

77. How do you select, collect, align, and integrate improving performance data and information for tracking daily operations and overall organizational performance, including progress relative to strategic objectives and action plans?
<--- Score

78. Are the improving performance standards challenging?
<--- Score

79. How will improving performance decisions be made and monitored?
<--- Score

80. What is your theory of human motivation, and how does your compensation plan fit with that view?
<--- Score

81. How will the day-to-day responsibilities for monitoring and continual improvement be transferred from the improvement team to the process owner?
<--- Score

82. How might the group capture best practices and lessons learned so as to leverage improvements?
<--- Score

83. Are the planned controls working?
<--- Score

84. What improving performance standards are applicable?
<--- Score

85. Can support from partners be adjusted?
<--- Score

86. Who is the improving performance process owner?
<--- Score

87. Is there a recommended audit plan for routine surveillance inspections of improving performance's gains?
<--- Score

88. What adjustments to the strategies are needed?
<--- Score

89. Has the improving performance value of standards been quantified?
<--- Score

90. How will the process owner and team be able to hold the gains?
<--- Score

91. Is there a documented and implemented monitoring plan?
<--- Score

92. What do your reports reflect?
<--- Score

93. What key inputs and outputs are being measured on an ongoing basis?
<--- Score

94. What is the best design framework for improving performance organization now that, in a post

industrial-age if the top-down, command and control model is no longer relevant?

<--- Score

95. Is a response plan established and deployed?

<--- Score

96. How will you measure your QA plan's effectiveness?

<--- Score

97. Have new or revised work instructions resulted?

<--- Score

98. Act/Adjust: What Do you Need to Do Differently?

<--- Score

99. In the case of a improving performance project, the criteria for the audit derive from implementation objectives, an audit of a improving performance project involves assessing whether the recommendations outlined for implementation have been met, can you track that any improving performance project is implemented as planned, and is it working?

<--- Score

100. What should you measure to verify efficiency gains?

<--- Score

101. What are the key elements of your improving performance performance improvement system, including your evaluation, organizational learning, and innovation processes?

<--- Score

Add up total points for this section:
_____ = Total points for this section

Divided by: _____ (number of
statements answered) = _____
Average score for this section

Transfer your score to the improving
performance Index at the beginning of
the Self-Assessment.

CRITERION #7: SUSTAIN:

INTENT: Retain the benefits.

In my belief, the answer to this question is clearly defined:

5 Strongly Agree

4 Agree

3 Neutral

2 Disagree

1 Strongly Disagree

1. What are the short and long-term improving performance goals?
<--- Score

2. Why should you adopt a improving performance framework?
<--- Score

3. What is the purpose of improving performance in relation to the mission?
<--- Score

4. If you had to rebuild your organization without any traditional competitive advantages (i.e., no killer technology, promising research, innovative product/service delivery model, etcetera), how would your people have to approach their work and collaborate together in order to create the necessary conditions for success?
<--- Score

5. What knowledge, skills and characteristics mark a good improving performance project manager?
<--- Score

6. Instead of going to current contacts for new ideas, what if you reconnected with dormant contacts-- the people you used to know? If you were going reactivate a dormant tie, who would it be?
<--- Score

7. How much does improving performance help?
<--- Score

8. What is something you believe that nearly no one agrees with you on?
<--- Score

9. Are assumptions made in improving performance stated explicitly?
<--- Score

10. How can you negotiate improving performance successfully with a stubborn boss, an irate client, or a deceitful coworker?
<--- Score

11. Is improving performance realistic, or are you setting yourself up for failure?
<--- Score

12. What role does communication play in the success or failure of a improving performance project?
<--- Score

13. How can you incorporate support to ensure safe and effective use of improving performance into the services that you provide?
<--- Score

14. Who will be responsible for deciding whether improving performance goes ahead or not after the initial investigations?
<--- Score

15. Is a improving performance team work effort in place?
<--- Score

16. How do senior leaders deploy your organizations vision and values through your leadership system, to the workforce, to key suppliers and partners, and to customers and other stakeholders, as appropriate?
<--- Score

17. Are you changing as fast as the world around you?
<--- Score

18. What was the last experiment you ran?
<--- Score

19. What is the craziest thing you can do?
<--- Score

20. To whom do you add value?
<--- Score

21. How do you cross-sell and up-sell your improving performance success?
<--- Score

22. What is your BATNA (best alternative to a negotiated agreement)?
<--- Score

23. What improving performance skills are most important?
<--- Score

24. Ask yourself: how would you do this work if you only had one staff member to do it?
<--- Score

25. What are the success criteria that will indicate that improving performance objectives have been met and the benefits delivered?
<--- Score

26. What is the kind of project structure that would be appropriate for your improving performance project, should it be formal and complex, or can it be less formal and relatively simple?
<--- Score

27. Why will customers want to buy your organizations products/services?
<--- Score

28. If you had to leave your organization for a year

and the only communication you could have with employees/colleagues was a single paragraph, what would you write?
<--- Score

29. What will be the consequences to the stakeholder (financial, reputation etc) if improving performance does not go ahead or fails to deliver the objectives?
<--- Score

30. Is your basic point _____ or _____?
<--- Score

31. Do improving performance rules make a reasonable demand on a users capabilities?
<--- Score

32. What are the gaps in your knowledge and experience?
<--- Score

33. What goals did you miss?
<--- Score

34. Is your strategy driving your strategy? Or is the way in which you allocate resources driving your strategy?
<--- Score

35. How do you accomplish your long range improving performance goals?
<--- Score

36. Is there any existing improving performance governance structure?
<--- Score

37. Do you think you know, or do you know you know ?
<--- Score

38. What could happen if you do not do it?
<--- Score

39. What is the source of the strategies for improving performance strengthening and reform?
<--- Score

40. What is the recommended frequency of auditing?
<--- Score

41. What are specific improving performance rules to follow?
<--- Score

42. What are the challenges?
<--- Score

43. In retrospect, of the projects that you pulled the plug on, what percent do you wish had been allowed to keep going, and what percent do you wish had ended earlier?
<--- Score

44. Are you paying enough attention to the partners your company depends on to succeed?
<--- Score

45. How do you manage improving performance Knowledge Management (KM)?
<--- Score

46. Who are your customers?
<--- Score

47. Would you rather sell to knowledgeable and informed customers or to uninformed customers?
<--- Score

48. What are the business goals improving performance is aiming to achieve?
<--- Score

49. How do you set improving performance stretch targets and how do you get people to not only participate in setting these stretch targets but also that they strive to achieve these?
<--- Score

50. Which models, tools and techniques are necessary?
<--- Score

51. Are you satisfied with your current role? If not, what is missing from it?
<--- Score

52. What are the rules and assumptions your industry operates under? What if the opposite were true?
<--- Score

53. How do you keep records, of what?
<--- Score

54. How long will it take to change?
<--- Score

55. What is your question? Why?

<--- Score

56. How do you listen to customers to obtain actionable information?
<--- Score

57. Who will provide the final approval of improving performance deliverables?
<--- Score

58. Who is the main stakeholder, with ultimate responsibility for driving improving performance forward?
<--- Score

59. What potential megatrends could make your business model obsolete?
<--- Score

60. Why not do improving performance?
<--- Score

61. What happens if you do not have enough funding?
<--- Score

62. What new services of functionality will be implemented next with improving performance ?
<--- Score

63. How do you ensure that implementations of improving performance products are done in a way that ensures safety?
<--- Score

64. What is effective improving performance?

<--- Score

65. Do you think improving performance accomplishes the goals you expect it to accomplish?
<--- Score

66. What is your formula for success in improving performance ?
<--- Score

67. What is your competitive advantage?
<--- Score

68. How do customers see your organization?
<--- Score

69. Are you relevant? Will you be relevant five years from now? Ten?
<--- Score

70. What happens when a new employee joins the organization?
<--- Score

71. How do you go about securing improving performance?
<--- Score

72. What unique value proposition (UVP) do you offer?
<--- Score

73. How can you become the company that would put you out of business?
<--- Score

74. How do you make it meaningful in connecting

improving performance with what users do day-to-day?
<--- Score

75. What trouble can you get into?
<--- Score

76. What threat is improving performance addressing?
<--- Score

77. Do you have enough freaky customers in your portfolio pushing you to the limit day in and day out?
<--- Score

78. How will you motivate the stakeholders with the least vested interest?
<--- Score

79. At what moment would you think; Will I get fired?
<--- Score

80. Are there any activities that you can take off your to do list?
<--- Score

81. In a project to restructure improving performance outcomes, which stakeholders would you involve?
<--- Score

82. Are you / should you be revolutionary or evolutionary?
<--- Score

83. Marketing budgets are tighter, consumers are more skeptical, and social media has changed forever the way we talk about improving performance, how

do you gain traction?
<--- Score

84. Are you making progress, and are you making progress as improving performance leaders?
<--- Score

85. Do you have past improving performance successes?
<--- Score

86. How do you determine the key elements that affect improving performance workforce satisfaction, how are these elements determined for different workforce groups and segments?
<--- Score

87. Who do you think the world wants your organization to be?
<--- Score

88. Can you maintain your growth without detracting from the factors that have contributed to your success?
<--- Score

89. What is the range of capabilities?
<--- Score

90. What are you trying to prove to yourself, and how might it be hijacking your life and business success?
<--- Score

91. How do you know if you are successful?
<--- Score

92. Will it be accepted by users?
<--- Score

93. Where can you break convention?
<--- Score

94. If your company went out of business tomorrow, would anyone who doesn't get a paycheck here care?
<--- Score

95. Which individuals, teams or departments will be involved in improving performance?
<--- Score

96. Can you break it down?
<--- Score

97. What are the potential basics of improving performance fraud?
<--- Score

98. What are the top 3 things at the forefront of your improving performance agendas for the next 3 years?
<--- Score

99. Who will determine interim and final deadlines?
<--- Score

100. Are you using a design thinking approach and integrating Innovation, improving performance Experience, and Brand Value?
<--- Score

101. What you are going to do to affect the numbers?
<--- Score

102. Who, on the executive team or the board, has spoken to a customer recently?
<--- Score

103. What does your signature ensure?
<--- Score

104. What would you recommend your friend do if he/she were facing this dilemma?
<--- Score

105. How do you assess the improving performance pitfalls that are inherent in implementing it?
<--- Score

106. What stupid rule would you most like to kill?
<--- Score

107. If there were zero limitations, what would you do differently?
<--- Score

108. Do you feel that more should be done in the improving performance area?
<--- Score

109. What would have to be true for the option on the table to be the best possible choice?
<--- Score

110. What relationships among improving performance trends do you perceive?
<--- Score

111. Do you have the right capabilities and capacities?
<--- Score

112. Is maximizing improving performance protection the same as minimizing improving performance loss?
<--- Score

113. How do you govern and fulfill your societal responsibilities?
<--- Score

114. What projects are going on in the organization today, and what resources are those projects using from the resource pools?
<--- Score

115. How do you proactively clarify deliverables and improving performance quality expectations?
<--- Score

116. Is there a work around that you can use?
<--- Score

117. What are you challenging?
<--- Score

118. Who else should you help?
<--- Score

119. Why should people listen to you?
<--- Score

120. Whose voice (department, ethnic group, women, older workers, etc) might you have missed hearing from in your company, and how might you amplify this voice to create positive momentum for your business?
<--- Score

121. How do you transition from the baseline to the target?
<--- Score

122. What are your personal philosophies regarding improving performance and how do they influence your work?
<--- Score

123. Do you say no to customers for no reason?
<--- Score

124. If you got fired and a new hire took your place, what would she do different?
<--- Score

125. How will you ensure you get what you expected?
<--- Score

126. What are the essentials of internal improving performance management?
<--- Score

127. What are internal and external improving performance relations?
<--- Score

128. How do you create buy-in?
<--- Score

129. Who do we want your customers to become?
<--- Score

130. Who is on the team?
<--- Score

131. If you were responsible for initiating and implementing major changes in your organization, what steps might you take to ensure acceptance of those changes?
<--- Score

132. What is the funding source for this project?
<--- Score

133. How important is improving performance to the user organizations mission?
<--- Score

134. Who do you want your customers to become?
<--- Score

135. Which functions and people interact with the supplier and or customer?
<--- Score

136. How do you foster innovation?
<--- Score

137. Are the assumptions believable and achievable?
<--- Score

138. Why do and why don't your customers like your organization?
<--- Score

139. How are you doing compared to your industry?
<--- Score

140. What are the barriers to increased improving performance production?

<--- Score

141. Are all key stakeholders present at all Structured Walkthroughs?
<--- Score

142. If you find that you havent accomplished one of the goals for one of the steps of the improving performance strategy, what will you do to fix it?
<--- Score

143. What management system can you use to leverage the improving performance experience, ideas, and concerns of the people closest to the work to be done?
<--- Score

144. Who will manage the integration of tools?
<--- Score

145. What information is critical to your organization that your executives are ignoring?
<--- Score

146. Who is responsible for errors?
<--- Score

147. How much contingency will be available in the budget?
<--- Score

148. Is it economical; do you have the time and money?
<--- Score

149. Whom among your colleagues do you trust, and

for what?
<--- Score

150. Think of your improving performance project, what are the main functions?
<--- Score

151. Do you know what you are doing? And who do you call if you don't?
<--- Score

152. What have you done to protect your business from competitive encroachment?
<--- Score

153. What is a feasible sequencing of reform initiatives over time?
<--- Score

154. What is the overall business strategy?
<--- Score

155. What are current improving performance paradigms?
<--- Score

156. What should you stop doing?
<--- Score

157. Do you have an implicit bias for capital investments over people investments?
<--- Score

158. What counts that you are not counting?
<--- Score

159. How do you lead with improving performance in mind?
<--- Score

160. What is the overall talent health of your organization as a whole at senior levels, and for each organization reporting to a member of the Senior Leadership Team?
<--- Score

161. What happens at your organization when people fail?
<--- Score

162. How do you engage the workforce, in addition to satisfying them?
<--- Score

163. How do you keep the momentum going?
<--- Score

164. Who is responsible for ensuring appropriate resources (time, people and money) are allocated to improving performance?
<--- Score

165. What did you miss in the interview for the worst hire you ever made?
<--- Score

166. Who is responsible for improving performance?
<--- Score

167. Who are four people whose careers you have enhanced?
<--- Score

168. Will there be any necessary staff changes (redundancies or new hires)?
<--- Score

169. How will you insure seamless interoperability of improving performance moving forward?
<--- Score

170. What are the usability implications of improving performance actions?
<--- Score

171. Can the schedule be done in the given time?
<--- Score

172. Is improving performance dependent on the successful delivery of a current project?
<--- Score

173. What are the long-term improving performance goals?
<--- Score

174. If you do not follow, then how to lead?
<--- Score

175. What one word do you want to own in the minds of your customers, employees, and partners?
<--- Score

176. How can you become more high-tech but still be high touch?
<--- Score

177. In the past year, what have you done (or could

you have done) to increase the accurate perception of your company/brand as ethical and honest?
<--- Score

178. What is it like to work for you?
<--- Score

179. What may be the consequences for the performance of an organization if all stakeholders are not consulted regarding improving performance?
<--- Score

180. What are the key enablers to make this improving performance move?
<--- Score

181. Who are the key stakeholders?
<--- Score

182. Is there any reason to believe the opposite of my current belief?
<--- Score

183. What is an unauthorized commitment?
<--- Score

184. How do you track customer value, profitability or financial return, organizational success, and sustainability?
<--- Score

185. Who have you, as a company, historically been when you've been at your best?
<--- Score

186. How is implementation research currently

incorporated into each of your goals?
<--- Score

187. What are strategies for increasing support and reducing opposition?
<--- Score

188. What are your most important goals for the strategic improving performance objectives?
<--- Score

189. Has implementation been effective in reaching specified objectives so far?
<--- Score

190. What is your improving performance strategy?
<--- Score

191. When information truly is ubiquitous, when reach and connectivity are completely global, when computing resources are infinite, and when a whole new set of impossibilities are not only possible, but happening, what will that do to your business?
<--- Score

192. How will you know that the improving performance project has been successful?
<--- Score

193. If your customer were your grandmother, would you tell her to buy what you're selling?
<--- Score

194. How do you stay inspired?
<--- Score

195. Which improving performance goals are the most important?
<--- Score

196. If you weren't already in this business, would you enter it today? And if not, what are you going to do about it?
<--- Score

197. How do you maintain improving performance's Integrity?
<--- Score

198. Can you do all this work?
<--- Score

199. Is the improving performance organization completing tasks effectively and efficiently?
<--- Score

200. What improving performance modifications can you make work for you?
<--- Score

201. If no one would ever find out about your accomplishments, how would you lead differently?
<--- Score

202. What business benefits will improving performance goals deliver if achieved?
<--- Score

Add up total points for this section:
_ _ _ _ _ = Total points for this section

Divided by: _ _ _ _ _ _ (number of

statements answered) = _ _ _ _ _ _
Average score for this section

Transfer your score to the improving performance Index at the beginning of the Self-Assessment.

Improving Performance and Managing Projects, Criteria for Project Managers:

1.0 Initiating Process Group: Improving Performance

1. How to control and approve each phase?

2. How will you do it?

3. How well defined and documented were the Improving Performance project management processes you chose to use?

4. What were things that you did well, and could improve, and how?

5. Are identified risks being monitored properly, are new risks arising during the Improving Performance project or are foreseen risks occurring?

6. What business situation is being addressed?

7. When are the deliverables to be generated in each phase?

8. Have you evaluated the teams performance and asked for feedback?

9. Specific - is the objective clear in terms of what, how, when, and where the situation will be changed?

10. Establishment of pm office?

11. Do you know if the Improving Performance project requires outside equipment or vendor resources?

12. Are the Improving Performance project team and stakeholders meeting regularly and using a meeting agenda and taking notes to accurately document what is being covered and what happened in the weekly meetings?

13. Information sharing?

14. Have requirements been tested, approved, and fulfill the Improving Performance project scope?

15. What communication items need improvement?

16. Although the Improving Performance project manager does not directly manage procurement and contracting activities, who does manage procurement and contracting activities in your organization then if not the PM?

17. During which stage of Risk planning are modeling techniques used to determine overall effects of risks on Improving Performance project objectives for high probability, high impact risks?

18. Are there resources to maintain and support the outcome of the Improving Performance project?

19. What are the short and long term implications?

20. What will you do?

1.1 Project Charter: Improving Performance

21. Market – identify products market, including whether it is outside of the objective: what is the purpose of the program or Improving Performance project?

22. Where does all this information come from?

23. What changes can you make to improve?

24. How much?

25. Are there special technology requirements?

26. How are Improving Performance projects different from operations?

27. What outcome, in measureable terms, are you hoping to accomplish?

28. Is it an improvement over existing products?

29. Why the improvements?

30. How will you know that a change is an improvement?

31. When?

32. Why is it important?

33. Who ise input and support will this Improving Performance project require?

34. What goes into your Improving Performance project Charter?

35. What material?

36. What does it need to do?

37. What are the constraints?

38. What are the known stakeholder requirements?

39. What metrics could you look at?

40. What are you trying to accomplish?

1.2 Stakeholder Register: Improving Performance

41. What are the major Improving Performance project milestones requiring communications or providing communications opportunities?

42. Is your organization ready for change?

43. What is the power of the stakeholder?

44. How will reports be created?

45. Who wants to talk about Security?

46. What opportunities exist to provide communications?

47. How should employers make voices heard?

48. Who is managing stakeholder engagement?

49. How much influence do they have on the Improving Performance project?

50. Who are the stakeholders?

51. What & Why?

52. How big is the gap?

1.3 Stakeholder Analysis Matrix: Improving Performance

53. What organizational arrangements are planned to ensure the Improving Performance project achieves its social development outcomes?

54. Organizational Applicability?

55. Why do you care?

56. Who will be affected by the Improving Performance project?

57. Accreditations, qualifications, certifications?

58. Which conditions out of the control of the management are crucial for the sustainability of its effects?

59. What mechanisms are proposed to monitor and measure Improving Performance project performance in terms of social development outcomes?

60. Who has been involved in the area (thematic or geographic) in the past?

61. How do you manage Improving Performance project Risk?

62. Sustaining internal capabilities?

63. What do you need to appraise?

64. Own known vulnerabilities?

65. Participatory approach: how will key stakeholders participate in the Improving Performance project?

66. Partnership opportunities/synergies?

67. Technology development and innovation?

68. Seasonality, weather effects?

69. Are you working on the right risks?

70. Who is influential in the Improving Performance project area (both thematic and geographic areas)?

71. What do you Evaluate?

72. What is your Advocacy Strategy?

2.0 Planning Process Group: Improving Performance

73. How does activity resource estimation affect activity duration estimation?

74. How will users learn how to use the deliverables?

75. Are you just doing busywork to pass the time?

76. If action is called for, what form should it take?

77. Do the partners have sufficient financial capacity to keep up the benefits produced by the programme?

78. Is the identification of the problems, inequalities and gaps, with respective causes, clear in the Improving Performance project?

79. Is the pace of implementing the products of the program ensuring the completeness of the results of the Improving Performance project?

80. To what extent and in what ways are the Improving Performance project contributing to progress towards organizational reform?

81. Did the program design/ implementation strategy adequately address the planning stage necessary to set up structures, hire staff etc.?

82. Is the schedule for the set products being met?

83. How well will the chosen processes produce the expected results?

84. What makes your Improving Performance project successful?

85. If task x starts two days late, what is the effect on the Improving Performance project end date?

86. In which Improving Performance project management process group is the detailed Improving Performance project budget created?

87. How do you integrate Improving Performance project Planning with the Iterative/Evolutionary SDLC?

88. What factors are contributing to progress or delay in the achievement of products and results?

89. In what ways can the governance of the Improving Performance project be improved so that it has greater likelihood of achieving future sustainability?

90. What do they need to know about the Improving Performance project?

91. If a risk event occurs, what will you do?

92. To what extent are the visions and actions of the partners consistent or divergent with regard to the program?

2.1 Project Management Plan: Improving Performance

93. Who manages integration?

94. What does management expect of PMs?

95. Is there anything you would now do differently on your Improving Performance project based on past experience?

96. What are the deliverables?

97. How do you manage time?

98. What data/reports/tools/etc. do your PMs need?

99. Was the peer (technical) review of the cost estimates duly coordinated with the cost estimate center of expertise and addressed in the review documentation and certification?

100. What would you do differently?

101. Is mitigation authorized or recommended?

102. Do the proposed changes from the Improving Performance project include any significant risks to safety?

103. What data/reports/tools/etc. do program managers need?

104. Is the budget realistic?

105. Development trends and opportunities. What if the positive direction and vision of your organization causes expected trends to change?

106. Are alternatives safe, functional, constructible, economical, reasonable and sustainable?

107. What are the assigned resources?

108. When is the Improving Performance project management plan created?

109. If the Improving Performance project is complex or scope is specialized, do you have appropriate and/ or qualified staff available to perform the tasks?

2.2 Scope Management Plan: Improving Performance

110. What are the risks that could significantly affect the resources needed for the Improving Performance project?

111. Where do scope management processes fit in?

112. Is there a Steering Committee in place?

113. Sensitivity analysis?

114. Are updated Improving Performance project time & resource estimates reasonable based on the current Improving Performance project stage?

115. Are milestone deliverables effectively tracked and compared to Improving Performance project plan?

116. Does the title convey to the reader the essence of the Improving Performance project?

117. Has the Improving Performance project scope been baselined?

118. Can each item be appropriately scheduled?

119. Have Improving Performance project success criteria been defined?

120. Is each item clearly and completely defined?

121. Are assumptions being identified, recorded, analyzed, qualified and closed?

122. How are you planning to maintain the scope baseline and how will you manage scope changes?

123. Function of the configuration control board?

124. Have reserves been created to address risks?

125. Are mitigation strategies identified?

126. Are trade-offs between accepting the risk and mitigating the risk identified?

127. Will anyone else be involved in verifying the deliverables?

2.3 Requirements Management Plan: Improving Performance

128. Is it new or replacing an existing business system or process?

129. Does the Improving Performance project have a Change Control process?

130. Is the user satisfied?

131. Is the change control process documented?

132. Should you include sub-activities?

133. What are you trying to do?

134. Who came up with this requirement?

135. Did you distinguish the scope of work the contractor(s) will be required to do?

136. Why manage requirements?

137. What are you counting on?

138. Describe the process for rejecting the Improving Performance project requirements. Who has the authority to reject Improving Performance project requirements?

139. What is the earliest finish date for this Improving Performance project if it is scheduled to start on ...?

140. Will the Improving Performance project requirements become approved in writing?

141. Do you have an appropriate arrangement for meetings?

142. Will you have access to stakeholders when you need them?

143. Will you use an assessment of the Improving Performance project environment as a tool to discover risk to the requirements process?

144. Is requirements work dependent on any other specific Improving Performance project or non-Improving Performance project activities (e.g. funding, approvals, procurement)?

145. When and how will a requirements baseline be established in this Improving Performance project?

146. Which hardware or software, related to, or as outcome of the Improving Performance project is new to your organization?

147. What cost metrics will be used?

2.4 Requirements Documentation: Improving Performance

148. Does the system provide the functions which best support the customers needs?

149. Can the requirements be checked?

150. Are there any requirements conflicts?

151. How will the proposed Improving Performance project help?

152. What are the potential disadvantages/ advantages?

153. Is your business case still valid?

154. Where are business rules being captured?

155. What happens when requirements are wrong?

156. How can you document system requirements?

157. What is the risk associated with cost and schedule?

158. Who is interacting with the system?

159. Are all functions required by the customer included?

160. Is the requirement properly understood?

161. What is the risk associated with the technology?

162. What marketing channels do you want to use: e-mail, letter or sms?

163. Who provides requirements?

164. If applicable; are there issues linked with the fact that this is an offshore Improving Performance project?

165. Does your organization restrict technical alternatives?

166. Is the requirement realistically testable?

167. What are current process problems?

2.5 Requirements Traceability Matrix: Improving Performance

168. How will it affect the stakeholders personally in career?

169. Is there a requirements traceability process in place?

170. Why use a WBS?

171. How do you manage scope?

172. What percentage of Improving Performance projects are producing traceability matrices between requirements and other work products?

173. What is the WBS?

174. What are the chronologies, contingencies, consequences, criteria?

175. Will you use a Requirements Traceability Matrix?

176. How small is small enough?

177. Describe the process for approving requirements so they can be added to the traceability matrix and Improving Performance project work can be performed. Will the Improving Performance project requirements become approved in writing?

178. Do you have a clear understanding of all

subcontracts in place?

179. Why do you manage scope?

2.6 Project Scope Statement: Improving Performance

180. Are there completion/verification criteria defined for each task producing an output?

181. Will statistics related to QA be collected, trends analyzed, and problems raised as issues?

182. Has the Improving Performance project scope statement been reviewed as part of the baseline process?

183. Write a brief purpose statement for this Improving Performance project. Include a business justification statement. What is the product of this Improving Performance project?

184. Will tasks be marked complete only after QA has been successfully completed?

185. Have you been able to thoroughly document the Improving Performance projects assumptions and constraints?

186. Is there an information system for the Improving Performance project?

187. What process would you recommend for creating the Improving Performance project scope statement?

188. Why do you need to manage scope?

189. Are there issues that could affect the existing requirements for the result, service, or product if the scope changes?

190. Have you been able to easily identify success criteria and create objective measurements for each of the Improving Performance project scopes goal statements?

191. What is change?

192. Have the configuration management functions been assigned?

193. What went right?

194. Will all Improving Performance project issues be unconditionally tracked through the issue resolution process?

195. Will an issue form be in use?

196. What actions will be taken to mitigate the risk?

197. Will you need a statement of work?

198. Did your Improving Performance project ask for this?

199. Will there be a Change Control Process in place?

2.7 Assumption and Constraint Log: Improving Performance

200. Violation trace: why ?

201. Are formal code reviews conducted?

202. Is staff trained on the software technologies that are being used on the Improving Performance project?

203. Are requirements management tracking tools and procedures in place?

204. What do you log?

205. Are there processes defining how software will be developed including development methods, overall timeline for development, software product standards, and traceability?

206. When can log be discarded?

207. No superfluous information or marketing narrative?

208. Model-building: what data-analytic strategies are useful when building proportional-hazards models?

209. Security analysis has access to information that is sanitized?

210. What strengths do you have?

211. Contradictory information between different documents?

212. Does the system design reflect the requirements?

213. Is the steering committee active in Improving Performance project oversight?

214. Have Improving Performance project management standards and procedures been established and documented?

215. What weaknesses do you have?

216. Have all stakeholders been identified?

217. Do the requirements meet the standards of correctness, completeness, consistency, accuracy, and readability?

218. What would you gain if you spent time working to improve this process?

2.8 Work Breakdown Structure: Improving Performance

219. Is it still viable?

220. When do you stop?

221. How much detail?

222. Is it a change in scope?

223. Is the work breakdown structure (wbs) defined and is the scope of the Improving Performance project clear with assigned deliverable owners?

224. What is the probability of completing the Improving Performance project in less that xx days?

225. How big is a work-package?

226. Can you make it?

227. How far down?

228. How will you and your Improving Performance project team define the Improving Performance projects scope and work breakdown structure?

229. Who has to do it?

230. Why is it useful?

231. How many levels?

232. When would you develop a Work Breakdown Structure?

233. What has to be done?

234. Why would you develop a Work Breakdown Structure?

235. When does it have to be done?

236. Where does it take place?

2.9 WBS Dictionary: Improving Performance

237. Are the requirements for all items of overhead established by rational, traceable processes?

238. Identify potential or actual budget-based and time-based schedule variances?

239. What is the goal?

240. Changes in the overhead pool and/or organization structures?

241. Are the overhead pools formally and adequately identified?

242. Are overhead cost budgets (or Improving Performance projections) established on a facility-wide basis at least annually for the life of the contract?

243. Are the wbs and organizational levels for application of the Improving Performance projected overhead costs identified?

244. All cwbs elements specified for external reporting?

245. Are all elements of indirect expense identified to overhead cost budgets of Improving Performance projections?

246. Cwbs elements to be subcontracted, with

identification of subcontractors?

247. Is subcontracted work defined and identified to the appropriate subcontractor within the proper WBS element?

248. Does the contractor have procedures which permit identification of recurring or non-recurring costs as necessary?

249. Is work properly classified as measured effort, LOE, or apportioned effort and appropriately separated?

250. Incurrence of actual indirect costs in excess of budgets, by element of expense?

251. Authorization to proceed with all authorized work?

252. Do work packages consist of discrete tasks which are adequately described?

253. How detailed should a Improving Performance project get?

2.10 Schedule Management Plan: Improving Performance

254. Are the activity durations realistic and at an appropriate level of detail for effective management?

255. Does the Improving Performance project have quality set of schedule BOEs?

256. Do Improving Performance project teams & team members report on status / activities / progress?

257. Is the critical path valid?

258. Cost / benefit analysis?

259. Is your organization certified as a supplier, wholesaler and/or regular dealer?

260. Is the ims used by all levels of management for Improving Performance project implementation and control?

261. Are post milestone Improving Performance project reviews (PMPR) conducted with your organization at least once a year?

262. Must the Improving Performance project be complete by a specified date?

263. Has the ims been resource-loaded and are assigned resources reasonable and available?

264. Improving Performance project definition & scope?

265. Are target dates established for each milestone deliverable?

266. What is the difference between % Complete and % work?

267. Is the correct WBS element identified for each task and milestone in the IMS?

268. Are the appropriate IT resources adequate to meet planned commitments?

269. Are software metrics formally captured, analyzed and used as a basis for other Improving Performance project estimates?

270. Are the results of quality assurance reviews provided to affected groups & individuals?

271. Is quality monitored from the perspective of the customers needs and expectations?

272. Are the people assigned to the Improving Performance project sufficiently qualified?

2.11 Activity List: Improving Performance

273. Is infrastructure setup part of your Improving Performance project?

274. What is your organizations history in doing similar activities?

275. What did not go as well?

276. How much slack is available in the Improving Performance project?

277. What is the LF and LS for each activity?

278. For other activities, how much delay can be tolerated?

279. When do the individual activities need to start and finish?

280. What went wrong?

281. The wbs is developed as part of a joint planning session. and how do you know that youhave done this right?

282. How can the Improving Performance project be displayed graphically to better visualize the activities?

283. How will it be performed?

284. How should ongoing costs be monitored to try to keep the Improving Performance project within budget?

285. Are the required resources available or need to be acquired?

286. How do you determine the late start (LS) for each activity?

287. When will the work be performed?

288. What went well?

289. How detailed should a Improving Performance project get?

290. Who will perform the work?

291. What will be performed?

2.12 Activity Attributes: Improving Performance

292. Would you consider either of corresponding activities an outlier?

293. Do you feel very comfortable with your prediction?

294. Have you identified the Activity Leveling Priority code value on each activity?

295. How difficult will it be to do specific activities on this Improving Performance project?

296. What conclusions/generalizations can you draw from this?

297. How difficult will it be to complete specific activities on this Improving Performance project?

298. What is the general pattern here?

299. Activity: what is Missing?

300. Where else does it apply?

301. Has management defined a definite timeframe for the turnaround or Improving Performance project window?

302. Can more resources be added?

303. Resources to accomplish the work?

304. Is there anything planned that does not need to be here?

305. What is missing?

306. Why?

307. Which method produces the more accurate cost assignment?

308. How many resources do you need to complete the work scope within a limit of X number of days?

2.13 Milestone List: Improving Performance

309. New USPs?

310. Calculate how long can activity be delayed?

311. Effects on core activities, distraction?

312. Can you derive how soon can the whole Improving Performance project finish?

313. Legislative effects?

314. Usps (unique selling points)?

315. How late can each activity be finished and started?

316. How soon can the activity finish?

317. What has been done so far?

318. Sustainable financial backing?

319. Loss of key staff?

320. Global influences?

321. How difficult will it be to do specific activities on this Improving Performance project?

322. Insurmountable weaknesses?

323. Identify critical paths (one or more) and which activities are on the critical path?

324. Do you foresee any technical risks or developmental challenges?

325. Obstacles faced?

326. Continuity, supply chain robustness?

2.14 Network Diagram: Improving Performance

327. What can be done concurrently?

328. What are the Major Administrative Issues?

329. What are the tools?

330. What job or jobs precede it?

331. Where do schedules come from?

332. What is the lowest cost to complete this Improving Performance project in xx weeks?

333. What must be completed before an activity can be started?

334. What controls the start and finish of a job?

335. What is the probability of completing the Improving Performance project in less that xx days?

336. Why must you schedule milestones, such as reviews, throughout the Improving Performance project?

337. What job or jobs could run concurrently?

338. What to do and When?

339. Where do you schedule uncertainty time?

340. Are the required resources available?

341. Are the gantt chart and/or network diagram updated periodically and used to assess the overall Improving Performance project timetable?

342. Will crashing x weeks return more in benefits than it costs?

343. Are you on time?

344. If the Improving Performance project network diagram cannot change and you have extra personnel resources, what is the BEST thing to do?

2.15 Activity Resource Requirements: Improving Performance

345. What is the Work Plan Standard?

346. How many signatures do you require on a check and does this match what is in your policy and procedures?

347. Anything else?

348. Why do you do that?

349. Are there unresolved issues that need to be addressed?

350. Other support in specific areas?

351. What are constraints that you might find during the Human Resource Planning process?

352. Do you use tools like decomposition and rolling-wave planning to produce the activity list and other outputs?

353. Time for overtime?

354. Which logical relationship does the PDM use most often?

355. How do you handle petty cash?

356. When does monitoring begin?

2.16 Resource Breakdown Structure: Improving Performance

357. What is Improving Performance project communication management?

358. How difficult will it be to do specific activities on this Improving Performance project?

359. Goals for the Improving Performance project. What is each stakeholders desired outcome for the Improving Performance project?

360. Who needs what information?

361. What is the number one predictor of a groups productivity?

362. Why do you do it?

363. Any changes from stakeholders?

364. What defines a successful Improving Performance project?

365. Who will be used as a Improving Performance project team member?

366. What can you do to improve productivity?

367. What are the requirements for resource data?

368. When do they need the information?

369. Is predictive resource analysis being done?

370. Why is this important?

2.17 Activity Duration Estimates: Improving Performance

371. What are the Improving Performance project management deliverables of each process group?

372. What are the advantages and disadvantages of PERT?

373. Improving Performance project manager has received activity duration estimates from his team. Which does one need in order to complete schedule development?

374. How can organizations use a weighted decision matrix to evaluate proposals as part of source selection?

375. Are risks monitored to determine if an event has occurred or if the mitigation was successful?

376. Is a contract developed which obligates the seller and the buyer?

377. When would a milestone chart be used instead of a bar char?

378. Which would be the NEXT thing for the Improving Performance project manager to do?

379. What type of people would you want on your team?

380. On which process should team members spend the most time?

381. Write a oneto two-page paper describing your dream team for this Improving Performance project. What type of people would you want on your team?

382. Do Improving Performance project team members work in the same physical location to enhance team performance?

383. Do you think Improving Performance project managers of large information technology Improving Performance projects need strong technical skills?

384. Do they make sense?

385. Is a contract change control system defined to manage changes to contract terms and conditions?

386. Will it help promote wellness at your organization and reduce insurance costs?

387. Improving Performance project manager is using weighted average duration estimates to perform schedule network analysis. Which type of mathematical analysis is being used?

388. Which is the BEST Improving Performance project management tool to use to determine the longest time the Improving Performance project will take?

389. Do you agree with the suggestions provided for improving Improving Performance project communications?

390. Does a procedure exist to ensure the Improving Performance project work is completed in the appropriate sequence and on time?

2.18 Duration Estimating Worksheet: Improving Performance

391. What are the critical bottleneck activities?

392. Is this operation cost effective?

393. Value pocket identification & quantification what are value pockets?

394. Done before proceeding with this activity or what can be done concurrently?

395. What is cost and Improving Performance project cost management?

396. Will the Improving Performance project collaborate with the local community and leverage resources?

397. Do any colleagues have experience with your organization and/or RFPs?

398. Is the Improving Performance project responsive to community need?

399. What questions do you have?

400. Why estimate costs?

401. When, then?

402. Does the Improving Performance project provide

innovative ways for stakeholders to overcome obstacles or deliver better outcomes?

403. When does your organization expect to be able to complete it?

404. What is the total time required to complete the Improving Performance project if no delays occur?

405. Why estimate time and cost?

406. What is your role?

2.19 Project Schedule: Improving Performance

407. How can you fix it?

408. Is the structure for tracking the Improving Performance project schedule well defined and assigned to a specific individual?

409. Did the final product meet or exceed user expectations?

410. Your best shot for providing estimations how complex/how much work does the activity require?

411. Meet requirements?

412. Month Improving Performance project take?

413. If you can not fix it, how do you do it differently?

414. Master Improving Performance project schedule?

415. How much slack is available in the Improving Performance project?

416. Have all Improving Performance project delays been adequately accounted for, communicated to all stakeholders and adjustments made in overall Improving Performance project schedule?

417. Activity charts and bar charts are graphical representations of a Improving Performance project

schedule ...how do they differ?

418. Are the original Improving Performance project schedule and budget realistic?

419. What does that mean?

420. Why do you think schedule issues often cause the most conflicts on Improving Performance projects?

421. Did the Improving Performance project come in on schedule?

422. How can you minimize or control changes to Improving Performance project schedules?

423. Verify that the update is accurate. Are all remaining durations correct?

424. What is the most mis-scheduled part of process?

2.20 Cost Management Plan: Improving Performance

425. Outside experts?

426. Is the structure for tracking the Improving Performance project schedule well defined and assigned to a specific individual?

427. Contracting method – what contracting method is to be used for the contracts?

428. Are internal Improving Performance project status meetings held at reasonable intervals?

429. Has the Improving Performance project scope been baselined?

430. Are change requests logged and managed?

431. Does all Improving Performance project documentation reside in a common repository for easy access?

432. Are written status reports provided on a designated frequent basis?

433. Forecasts – how will the time and resources needed to complete the Improving Performance project be forecast?

434. Resources – how will human resources be scheduled during each phase of the Improving

Performance project?

435. Ranged estimates?

436. For cost control purposes?

437. What would you do differently what did not work?

438. Does the detailed work plan match the complexity of tasks with the capabilities of personnel?

439. Cost tracking and performance analysis – How will cost tracking and performance analysis be accomplished?

440. Does the schedule include Improving Performance project management time and change request analysis time?

441. Does the Improving Performance project have a formal Improving Performance project Charter?

442. Is there an approved case?

443. What is your organizations history in doing similar tasks?

2.21 Activity Cost Estimates: Improving Performance

444. What is included in indirect cost being allocated?

445. What do you want to know about the stay to know if costs were inappropriately high or low?

446. Does the estimator have experience?

447. How difficult will it be to do specific tasks on the Improving Performance project?

448. Were the costs or charges reasonable?

449. What is the activity inventory?

450. Who & what determines the need for contracted services?

451. What is the last item a Improving Performance project manager must do to finalize Improving Performance project close-out?

452. Were sponsors and decision makers available when needed outside regularly scheduled meetings?

453. What areas does the group agree are the biggest success on the Improving Performance project?

454. Based on your Improving Performance project communication management plan, what worked well?

455. How do you do activity recasts?

456. Does the estimator estimate by task or by person?

457. Was the consultant knowledgeable about the program?

458. How do you allocate indirect costs to activities?

459. What is the Improving Performance projects sustainability strategy that will ensure Improving Performance project results will endure or be sustained?

460. What areas were overlooked on this Improving Performance project?

461. How do you change activities?

462. How do you treat administrative costs in the activity inventory?

2.22 Cost Estimating Worksheet: Improving Performance

463. What will others want?

464. What is the purpose of estimating?

465. Identify the timeframe necessary to monitor progress and collect data to determine how the selected measure has changed?

466. How will the results be shared and to whom?

467. Ask: are others positioned to know, are others credible, and will others cooperate?

468. What info is needed?

469. Is the Improving Performance project responsive to community need?

470. What costs are to be estimated?

471. Who is best positioned to know and assist in identifying corresponding factors?

472. What is the estimated labor cost today based upon this information?

473. What can be included?

474. Is it feasible to establish a control group arrangement?

475. What happens to any remaining funds not used?

476. Does the Improving Performance project provide innovative ways for stakeholders to overcome obstacles or deliver better outcomes?

477. What additional Improving Performance project(s) could be initiated as a result of this Improving Performance project?

478. Can a trend be established from historical performance data on the selected measure and are the criteria for using trend analysis or forecasting methods met?

479. Will the Improving Performance project collaborate with the local community and leverage resources?

2.23 Cost Baseline: Improving Performance

480. Is there anything unique in this Improving Performance projects scope statement that will affect resources?

481. How will cost estimates be used?

482. Are you asking management for something as a result of this update?

483. What do you want to measure ?

484. Does it impact schedule, cost, quality?

485. Is there anything you need from upper management in order to be successful?

486. Has the appropriate access to relevant data and analysis capability been granted?

487. Verify business objectives. Are others appropriate, and well-articulated?

488. What is the reality?

489. Does the suggested change request represent a desired enhancement to the products functionality?

490. Does the suggested change request seem to represent a necessary enhancement to the product?

491. Why do you manage cost?

492. Have the lessons learned been filed with the Improving Performance project Management Office?

493. What threats might prevent you from getting there?

494. Have all approved changes to the Improving Performance project requirement been identified and impact on the performance, cost, and schedule baselines documented?

495. How do you manage cost?

496. Will the Improving Performance project fail if the change request is not executed?

2.24 Quality Management Plan: Improving Performance

497. What does it do for you (or to me)?

498. How is the information recorded?

499. How are records kept in the office?

500. What type of in-house testing do you conduct?

501. Methodology followed?

502. Documented results available?

503. Do you periodically review your data quality system to see that it is up to date and appropriate?

504. Who gets results of work?

505. Who is approving the QAPP?

506. How are your organizations compensation and recognition approaches and the performance management system used to reinforce high performance?

507. When reporting to different audiences, do you vary the form or type of report?

508. How does your organization manage training and evaluate its effectiveness?

509. How do you ensure that your sampling methods and procedures meet your data needs?

510. What data do you gather/use/compile?

511. Do you keep back-up copies of any data?

512. What changes can you make that will result in improvement?

513. Diagrams and tables to account for complex concepts and increase overall readability?

514. How does your organization maintain a safe and healthy work environment?

515. How do you decide what information needs to be recorded?

516. Are you meeting your customers expectations consistently?

2.25 Quality Metrics: Improving Performance

517. What is the timeline to meet your goal?

518. Has risk analysis been adequately reviewed?

519. What approved evidence based screening tools can be used?

520. Who notifies stakeholders of normal and abnormal results?

521. What documentation is required?

522. What happens if you get an abnormal result?

523. How are requirements conflicts resolved?

524. Did the team meet the Improving Performance project success criteria documented in the Quality Metrics Matrix?

525. Which data do others need in one place to target areas of improvement?

526. Do the operators focus on determining; is there anything you need to worry about?

527. What method of measurement do you use?

528. How can the effectiveness of each of the activities be measured?

529. Did evaluation start on time?

530. What metrics do you measure?

531. Who is willing to lead?

532. How effective are your security tests?

533. Can visual measures help you to filter visualizations of interest?

534. Does risk analysis documentation meet standards?

535. Are quality metrics defined?

536. What metrics are important and most beneficial to measure?

2.26 Process Improvement Plan: Improving Performance

537. Does your process ensure quality?

538. Are you meeting the quality standards?

539. Where do you focus?

540. What personnel are the sponsors for that initiative?

541. Who should prepare the process improvement action plan?

542. What is quality and how will you ensure it?

543. Why do you want to achieve the goal?

544. What is the test-cycle concept?

545. Have storage and access mechanisms and procedures been determined?

546. Are you making progress on your improvement plan?

547. Has the time line required to move measurement results from the points of collection to databases or users been established?

548. Are you making progress on the goals?

549. What actions are needed to address the problems and achieve the goals?

550. Are you following the quality standards?

551. How do you manage quality?

552. Purpose of goal: the motive is determined by asking, why do you want to achieve this goal?

553. Have the frequency of collection and the points in the process where measurements will be made been determined?

554. To elicit goal statements, do you ask a question such as, What do you want to achieve?

555. If a process improvement framework is being used, which elements will help the problems and goals listed?

556. Has a process guide to collect the data been developed?

2.27 Responsibility Assignment Matrix: Improving Performance

557. The staff interests – is the group or the person interested in working for this Improving Performance project?

558. Budgets assigned to major functional organizations?

559. Wbs elements contractually specified for reporting of status (lowest level only)?

560. Not any rs, as, or cs: if an identified role is only informed, should others be eliminated from the matrix?

561. How do you assist them to be as productive as possible?

562. How can this help you with team building?

563. Does each role with Accountable responsibility have the authority within your organization to make the required decisions?

564. What do you do when people do not respond?

565. Changes in the current direct and Improving Performance projected base?

566. When performing is split among two or more roles, is the work clearly defined so that the efforts are

coordinated and the communication is clear?

567. Are indirect costs accumulated for comparison with the corresponding budgets?

568. Improving Performance projected economic escalation?

569. How cost benefit analysis?

570. Are meaningful indicators identified for use in measuring the status of cost and schedule performance?

571. Detailed schedules which support control account and work package start and completion dates/events?

572. Are work packages assigned to performing organizations?

573. What tool can show you individual and group allocations?

2.28 Roles and Responsibilities: Improving Performance

574. Does your vision/mission support a culture of quality data?

575. Do the values and practices inherent in the culture of your organization foster or hinder the process?

576. What expectations were met?

577. What should you highlight for improvement?

578. What is working well within your organizations performance management system?

579. Who is responsible for implementation activities and where will the functions, roles and responsibilities be defined?

580. Who: who is involved?

581. Authority: what areas/Improving Performance projects in your work do you have the authority to decide upon and act on the already stated decisions?

582. Required skills, knowledge, experience?

583. Accountabilities: what are the roles and responsibilities of individual team members?

584. Is feedback clearly communicated and non-

judgmental?

585. Is there a training program in place for stakeholders covering expectations, roles and responsibilities and any addition knowledge others need to be good stakeholders?

586. Are your budgets supportive of a culture of quality data?

587. Was the expectation clearly communicated?

588. What specific behaviors did you observe?

589. Is the data complete?

590. Attainable / achievable: the goal is attainable; can you actually accomplish the goal?

591. Key conclusions and recommendations: Are conclusions and recommendations relevant and acceptable?

592. Are Improving Performance project team roles and responsibilities identified and documented?

593. Are governance roles and responsibilities documented?

2.29 Human Resource Management Plan: Improving Performance

594. Is the manpower level sufficient to meet the future business requirements?

595. Are there checklists created to determine if all quality processes are followed?

596. Does a documented Improving Performance project organizational policy & plan (i.e. governance model) exist?

597. Has a capability assessment been conducted?

598. Were Improving Performance project team members involved in the development of activity & task decomposition?

599. Are Improving Performance project contact logs kept up to date?

600. Are decisions captured in a decisions log?

601. Do Improving Performance project managers participating in the Improving Performance project know the Improving Performance projects true status first hand?

602. How are you going to ensure that you have a well motivated workforce?

603. Are multiple estimation methods being

employed?

604. Was the scope definition used in task sequencing?

605. How do you determine what key skills and talents are needed to meet the objectives. Is your organization primarily focused on a specific industry?

606. Is there a formal process for updating the Improving Performance project baseline?

607. How complete is the human resource management plan?

608. Is your organization human?

609. Has a structured approach been used to break work effort into manageable components (WBS)?

610. Are cause and effect determined for risks when others occur?

2.30 Communications Management Plan: Improving Performance

611. Who is the stakeholder?

612. How do you manage communications?

613. How often do you engage with stakeholders?

614. Do you feel a register helps?

615. How will the person responsible for executing the communication item be notified?

616. How did the term stakeholder originate?

617. What to know?

618. Can you think of other people who might have concerns or interests?

619. Are you constantly rushing from meeting to meeting?

620. What is Improving Performance project communications management?

621. Conflict resolution -which method when?

622. What is the political influence?

623. How were corresponding initiatives successful?

624. Are stakeholders internal or external?

625. In your work, how much time is spent on stakeholder identification?

626. Is there an important stakeholder who is actively opposed and will not receive messages?

627. Is the stakeholder role recognized by your organization?

628. Are there too many who have an interest in some aspect of your work?

629. What does the stakeholder need from the team?

630. Are others part of the communications management plan?

2.31 Risk Management Plan: Improving Performance

631. Why is product liability a serious issue?

632. Have customers been involved fully in the definition of requirements?

633. Workarounds are determined during which step of risk management?

634. Is the technology to be built new to your organization?

635. Is the necessary data being captured and is it complete and accurate?

636. How can the process be made more effective or less cumbersome (process improvements)?

637. How do you manage Improving Performance project Risk?

638. Are there new risks that mitigation strategies might introduce?

639. What will the damage be?

640. How is implementation of risk actions performed?

641. Why do you want risk management?

642. Does the customer have a solid idea of what is required?

643. Are the best people available?

644. Who has experience with this?

645. How risk averse are you?

646. Are the metrics meaningful and useful?

647. Are the reports useful and easy to read?

648. Are you on schedule?

2.32 Risk Register: Improving Performance

649. Are your objectives at risk?

650. Who is going to do it?

651. Risk documentation: what reporting formats and processes will be used for risk management activities?

652. Assume the risk event or situation happens, what would the impact be?

653. What has changed since the last period?

654. How are risks identified?

655. What can be done about it?

656. Who needs to know about this?

657. Market risk -will the new service or product be useful to your organization or marketable to others?

658. Severity Prediction?

659. Are there any gaps in the evidence?

660. How well are risks controlled?

661. Can the likelihood and impact of failing to achieve corresponding recommendations and action plans be assessed?

662. Does the evidence highlight any areas to advance opportunities or foster good relations. If yes what steps will be taken?

663. How is a Community Risk Register created?

664. What are the main aims, objectives of the policy, strategy, or service and the intended outcomes?

665. What are the assumptions and current status that support the assessment of the risk?

666. Have other controls and solutions been implemented in other services which could be applied as an alternative to additional funding?

667. What is a Risk?

2.33 Probability and Impact Assessment: Improving Performance

668. What are the likely future requirements?

669. What are your data sources?

670. What will be cost of redeployment of personnel?

671. Are enough people available?

672. How do the products attain the specifications?

673. Who should be responsible for the monitoring and tracking of the indicators youhave identified?

674. What is the experience (performance, attitude, business ethics, etc.) in the past with contractors?

675. Have you worked with the customer in the past?

676. Are staff committed for the duration of the Improving Performance project?

677. Are tool mentors available?

678. Are flexibility and reuse paramount?

679. What risks are necessary to achieve success?

680. Do you use any methods to analyze risks?

681. Is the present organizational structure for

handling the Improving Performance project sufficient?

682. How is the Improving Performance project going to be managed?

683. What is the likelihood?

684. How carefully have the potential competitors been identified?

685. What is the risk appetite?

2.34 Probability and Impact Matrix: Improving Performance

686. Are team members trained in the use of the tools?

687. Do you know the order of planning yet?

688. Which phase of the Improving Performance project do you take part in?

689. How would you suggest monitoring for risk transition indicators?

690. What is the likely future demand of the customer?

691. During Improving Performance project executing, a team member identifies a risk that is not in the risk register. What should you do?

692. Amount of reused software?

693. Are formal technical reviews part of this process?

694. Brain storm – mind maps, what if?

695. Costs associated with late delivery or a defective product?

696. How is the risk management process used in practice?

697. What is the level of experience available with your organization?

698. What are the levels of understanding of the future users of this technology?

699. What should you do FIRST?

700. Have staff received necessary training?

701. Are the risk data complete?

702. Are testing tools available and suitable?

2.35 Risk Data Sheet: Improving Performance

703. How can it happen?

704. Potential for recurrence?

705. What can happen?

706. If it happens, what are the consequences?

707. What is the chance that it will happen?

708. Is the data sufficiently specified in terms of the type of failure being analyzed, and its frequency or probability?

709. What are the main opportunities available to you that you should grab while you can?

710. Who has a vested interest in how you perform as your organization (our stakeholders)?

711. What were the Causes that contributed?

712. Whom do you serve (customers)?

713. What are you trying to achieve (Objectives)?

714. What will be the consequences if the risk happens?

715. What are your core values?

716. Risk of what?

717. Will revised controls lead to tolerable risk levels?

718. Has the most cost-effective solution been chosen?

719. Has a sensitivity analysis been carried out?

2.36 Procurement Management Plan: Improving Performance

720. Has the Improving Performance project scope been baselined?

721. Is there a Quality Management Plan?

722. Has a Improving Performance project Communications Plan been developed?

723. Are meeting minutes captured and sent out after meetings?

724. In which phase of the Acquisition Process Cycle does source qualifications reside?

725. Has a quality assurance plan been developed for the Improving Performance project?

726. Is it standard practice to formally commit stakeholders to the Improving Performance project via agreements?

727. Have external dependencies been captured in the schedule?

728. Is documentation created for communication with the suppliers and Vendors?

729. Are non-critical path items updated and agreed upon with the teams?

730. Are staff skills known and available for each task?

731. Is the Improving Performance project sponsor clearly communicating the business case or rationale for why this Improving Performance project is needed?

732. Have all involved Improving Performance project stakeholders and work groups committed to the Improving Performance project?

733. What were things that you did very well and want to do the same again on the next Improving Performance project?

734. Is there a requirements change management processes in place?

735. Have the procedures for identifying budget variances been followed?

736. Is Improving Performance project work proceeding in accordance with the original Improving Performance project schedule?

737. Does the Improving Performance project team have the right skills?

2.37 Source Selection Criteria: Improving Performance

738. Have all evaluators been trained?

739. Are considerations anticipated?

740. Who should attend debriefings?

741. What should be considered when developing evaluation standards?

742. Do you want to wait until all offerors have been evaluated?

743. Have team members been adequately trained?

744. What will you use to capture evaluation and subsequent documentation?

745. When should debriefings be held and how should they be scheduled?

746. What evidence should be provided regarding proposal evaluations?

747. In the technical/management area, what criteria do you use to determine the final evaluation ratings?

748. What does a sample rating scale look like?

749. What are the steps in performing a cost/tech tradeoff?

750. Can you make a cost/technical tradeoff?

751. Who is entitled to a debriefing?

752. When is it appropriate to issue a Draft Request for Proposal (DRFP)?

753. How can solicitation Schedules be improved to yield more effective price competition?

754. Are types/quantities of material, facilities appropriate?

755. How should the solicitation aspects regarding past performance be structured?

756. With the rapid changes in information technology, will media be readable in five or ten years?

2.38 Stakeholder Management Plan: Improving Performance

757. Have activity relationships and interdependencies within tasks been adequately identified?

758. Are meeting objectives identified for each meeting?

759. Were Improving Performance project team members involved in detailed estimating and scheduling?

760. Are tasks tracked by hours?

761. How are the overall Improving Performance project development processes to be undertaken to produce the Improving Performance project outputs?

762. Is the communication plan being followed?

763. Were the budget estimates reasonable?

764. Are all resource assumptions documented?

765. Has a provision been made to reassess Improving Performance project risks at various Improving Performance project stages?

766. Are vendor invoices audited for accuracy before payment?

767. Was your organizations estimating methodology being used and followed?

768. Has the Improving Performance project manager been identified?

769. Alignment to strategic goals & objectives?

770. Have all necessary approvals been obtained?

771. Does the plan conform to standards?

772. Are procurement deliverables arriving on time and to specification?

773. Are post milestone Improving Performance project reviews (PMPR) conducted with your organization at least once a year?

774. Contradictory information between document sections?

775. Have all documents been archived in a Improving Performance project repository for each release?

2.39 Change Management Plan: Improving Performance

776. Is a training information sheet available?

777. What relationships will change?

778. What communication network would you use – informal or formal?

779. What are the responsibilities assigned to each role?

780. Does this change represent a completely new process for your organization, or a different application of an existing process?

781. Has the relevant business unit been notified of installation and support requirements?

782. Have the business unit contacts been briefed by the Improving Performance project team?

783. What prerequisite knowledge do corresponding groups need?

784. What are the needs, priorities and special interests of the audience?

785. Are there any restrictions on who can receive the communications?

786. What are the major changes to processes?

787. Has the target training audience been identified and nominated?

788. What are the key change management success metrics?

789. Do the proposed users have access to the appropriate documentation?

790. Who might present the most resistance?

791. What risks may occur upfront?

792. Do you need a new organization structure?

793. What new behaviours are required?

794. Has a training need analysis been carried out?

3.0 Executing Process Group: Improving Performance

795. What are the main processes included in Improving Performance project quality management?

796. How do you prevent staff are just doing busywork to pass the time?

797. Who are the Improving Performance project stakeholders?

798. How does Improving Performance project management relate to other disciplines?

799. What is the product of your Improving Performance project?

800. What is the difference between using brainstorming and the Delphi technique for risk identification?

801. Does the case present a realistic scenario?

802. How could stakeholders negatively impact your Improving Performance project?

803. What were things that you need to improve?

804. What are the typical Improving Performance project management skills?

805. What are the main types of goods and services

being outsourced?

806. What are the main parts of the scope statement?

807. How do you enter durations, link tasks, and view critical path information?

808. How can software assist in Improving Performance project communications?

809. What does it mean to take a systems view of a Improving Performance project?

810. How can your organization use a weighted decision matrix to evaluate proposals as part of source selection?

3.1 Team Member Status Report: Improving Performance

811. How will resource planning be done?

812. Are the products of your organizations Improving Performance projects meeting customers objectives?

813. Why is it to be done?

814. Does every department have to have a Improving Performance project Manager on staff?

815. How can you make it practical?

816. Does the product, good, or service already exist within your organization?

817. Does your organization have the means (staff, money, contract, etc.) to produce or to acquire the product, good, or service?

818. Do you have an Enterprise Improving Performance project Management Office (EPMO)?

819. When a teams productivity and success depend on collaboration and the efficient flow of information, what generally fails them?

820. What is to be done?

821. Are the attitudes of staff regarding Improving Performance project work improving?

822. What specific interest groups do you have in place?

823. How does this product, good, or service meet the needs of the Improving Performance project and your organization as a whole?

824. Is there evidence that staff is taking a more professional approach toward management of your organizations Improving Performance projects?

825. How it is to be done?

826. Will the staff do training or is that done by a third party?

827. How much risk is involved?

828. Are your organizations Improving Performance projects more successful over time?

829. The problem with Reward & Recognition Programs is that the truly deserving people all too often get left out. How can you make it practical?

3.2 Change Request: Improving Performance

830. How is quality being addressed on the Improving Performance project?

831. For which areas does this operating procedure apply?

832. Screen shots or attachments included in a Change Request?

833. Why do you want to have a change control system?

834. Who is responsible to authorize changes?

835. Who can suggest changes?

836. Who is included in the change control team?

837. Are there requirements attributes that are strongly related to the occurrence of defects and failures?

838. Have scm procedures for noting the change, recording it, and reporting it been followed?

839. Will all change requests and current status be logged?

840. What are the duties of the change control team?

841. What is the purpose of change control?

842. How are changes graded and who is responsible for the rating?

843. What kind of information about the change request needs to be captured?

844. What is the relationship between requirements attributes and attributes like complexity and size?

845. Why control change across the life cycle?

846. Who needs to approve change requests?

847. Describe how modifications, enhancements, defects and/or deficiencies shall be notified (e.g. Problem Reports, Change Requests etc) and managed. Detail warranty and/or maintenance periods?

848. Has the change been highlighted and documented in the CSCI?

849. Should a more thorough impact analysis be conducted?

3.3 Change Log: Improving Performance

850. Is the requested change request a result of changes in other Improving Performance project(s)?

851. Do the described changes impact on the integrity or security of the system?

852. How does this change affect the timeline of the schedule?

853. Where do changes come from?

854. Is the submitted change a new change or a modification of a previously approved change?

855. Will the Improving Performance project fail if the change request is not executed?

856. How does this relate to the standards developed for specific business processes?

857. Is the change request open, closed or pending?

858. When was the request approved?

859. Is the change request within Improving Performance project scope?

860. When was the request submitted?

861. How does this change affect scope?

862. Is the change backward compatible without limitations?

863. Is this a mandatory replacement?

864. Who initiated the change request?

3.4 Decision Log: Improving Performance

865. How does an increasing emphasis on cost containment influence the strategies and tactics used?

866. What is the line where eDiscovery ends and document review begins?

867. What alternatives/risks were considered?

868. Behaviors; what are guidelines that the team has identified that will assist them with getting the most out of team meetings?

869. Which variables make a critical difference?

870. Who will be given a copy of this document and where will it be kept?

871. Decision-making process; how will the team make decisions?

872. It becomes critical to track and periodically revisit both operational effectiveness; Are you noticing all that you need to, and are you interpreting what you see effectively?

873. How effective is maintaining the log at facilitating organizational learning?

874. How does the use a Decision Support System

influence the strategies/tactics or costs?

875. Is your opponent open to a non-traditional workflow, or will it likely challenge anything you do?

876. With whom was the decision shared or considered?

877. What are the cost implications?

878. Who is the decisionmaker?

879. How do you know when you are achieving it?

880. What was the rationale for the decision?

881. What is your overall strategy for quality control / quality assurance procedures?

882. What eDiscovery problem or issue did your organization set out to fix or make better?

883. Does anything need to be adjusted?

884. Do strategies and tactics aimed at less than full control reduce the costs of management or simply shift the cost burden?

3.5 Quality Audit: Improving Performance

885. Are there appropriate indicators for monitoring the effectiveness and efficiency of processes?

886. How does your organization know that its risk management system is appropriately effective and constructive?

887. Why are you trying to do it?

888. Can your organization demonstrate exactly how and why results were achieved?

889. What experience do staff have in the type of work that the audit entails?

890. How does your organization know that its staffing profile is optimally aligned with the capability requirements implicit (or explicit) in its Strategic Plan?

891. How does your organization know that its system for commercializing research outputs is appropriately effective and constructive?

892. Are the policies and processes, as set out in the Quality Audit Manual, properly applied?

893. Do the suppliers use a formal quality system?

894. How does your organization know that the range and quality of its social and recreational services and

facilities are appropriately effective and constructive in meeting the needs of staff?

895. Are multiple statements on the same issue consistent with each other?

896. How does your organization know that the system for managing its facilities is appropriately effective and constructive?

897. Health and safety arrangements; stress management workshops. How does your organization know that it provides a safe and healthy environment?

898. Is refuse and garbage adequately stored and disposed of with sufficient frequency to prevent contamination?

899. Is quality audit a prerequisite for program accreditation or program recognition?

900. How does your organization know that its system for managing intellectual property issues is appropriately effective, constructive and fair?

901. How does your organization know that its systems for providing high quality consultancy services to external parties are appropriately effective and constructive?

902. How does your organization know that its systems for communicating with and among staff are appropriately effective and constructive?

903. How does your organization know that its system for supporting staff research capability is

appropriately effective and constructive?

904. Is there a risk that information provided by management may not always be reliable?

3.6 Team Directory: Improving Performance

905. Who are the Team Members?

906. How will you accomplish and manage the objectives?

907. Who should receive information (all stakeholders)?

908. When will you produce deliverables?

909. Have you decided when to celebrate the Improving Performance projects completion date?

910. When does information need to be distributed?

911. Process decisions: which organizational elements and which individuals will be assigned management functions?

912. What needs to be communicated?

913. Is construction on schedule?

914. Process decisions: do job conditions warrant additional actions to collect job information and document on-site activity?

915. Who is the Sponsor?

916. Who are your stakeholders (customers, sponsors,

end users, team members)?

917. Why is the work necessary?

918. Who will talk to the customer?

919. Contract requirements complied with?

920. Who will write the meeting minutes and distribute?

921. Where should the information be distributed?

922. Days from the time the issue is identified?

923. Who will report Improving Performance project status to all stakeholders?

924. Who will be the stakeholders on your next Improving Performance project?

3.7 Team Operating Agreement: Improving Performance

925. What are some potential sources of conflict among team members?

926. Seconds for members to respond?

927. Do team members reside in more than two countries?

928. Do you ask participants to close laptops and place mobile devices on silent on the table while the meeting is in progress?

929. What are the safety issues/risks that need to be addressed and/or that the team needs to consider?

930. Do you post meeting notes and the recording (if used) and notify participants?

931. Are leadership responsibilities shared among team members (versus a single leader)?

932. What are the current caseload numbers in the unit?

933. What are the boundaries (organizational or geographic) within which you operate?

934. Does your team need access to all documents and information at all times?

935. The method to be used in the decision making process; Will it be consensus, majority rule, or the supervisor having the final say?

936. To whom do you deliver your services?

937. How will group handle unplanned absences?

938. Are there more than two native languages represented by your team?

939. Do you brief absent members after they view meeting notes or listen to a recording?

940. How does teaming fit in with overall organizational goals and meet organizational needs?

941. How will you resolve conflict efficiently and respectfully?

3.8 Team Performance Assessment: Improving Performance

942. Social categorization and intergroup behaviour: Does minimal intergroup discrimination make social identity more positive?

943. What is method variance?

944. To what degree do team members articulate the teams work approach?

945. To what degree do all members feel responsible for all agreed-upon measures?

946. What are you doing specifically to develop the leaders around you?

947. To what degree does the teams work approach provide opportunity for members to engage in fact-based problem solving?

948. To what degree are sub-teams possible or necessary?

949. To what degree does the teams work approach provide opportunity for members to engage in open interaction?

950. What structural changes have you made or are you preparing to make?

951. To what degree are corresponding categories of

skills either actually or potentially represented across the membership?

952. To what degree do team members feel that the purpose of the team is important, if not exciting?

953. To what degree are staff involved as partners in the improvement process?

954. To what degree do team members understand one anothers roles and skills?

955. To what degree is the team cognizant of small wins to be celebrated along the way?

956. To what degree are the teams goals and objectives clear, simple, and measurable?

957. Do friends perform better than acquaintances?

958. To what degree can team members vigorously define the teams purpose in considerations with others who are not part of the functioning team?

959. How hard do you try to make a good selection?

960. Do you promptly inform members about major developments that may affect them?

961. How much interpersonal friction is there in your team?

3.9 Team Member Performance Assessment: Improving Performance

962. Which training platform formats (i.e., mobile, virtual, videogame-based) were implemented in your effort(s)?

963. What kinds of performance factors / elements do you use?

964. What are the staffs preferences for training on technology-based platforms?

965. What is used as a basis for instructional decisions?

966. How do you currently use the time that is available?

967. To what degree is there a sense that only the team can succeed?

968. To what degree can all members engage in open and interactive considerations?

969. What happens if a team member receives a Rating of Unsatisfactory?

970. How should adaptive assessments be implemented?

971. How does your team work together?

972. What future plans (e.g., modifications) do you have for your program?

973. What evidence supports your decision-making?

974. Does the rater (supervisor) have to wait for the interim or final performance assessment review to tell an employee that the employees performance is unsatisfactory?

975. Does the rater (supervisor) have the authority or responsibility to tell an employee that the employees performance is unsatisfactory?

976. Is it critical or vital to the job?

977. What changes do you need to make to align practices with beliefs?

978. In what areas would you like to concentrate your knowledge and resources?

979. What resources do you need?

980. How is performance assessment used in making future award decisions including options and extend/compete decisions?

3.10 Issue Log: Improving Performance

981. Is access to the Issue Log controlled?

982. Who have you worked with in past, similar initiatives?

983. Is the issue log kept in a safe place?

984. In classifying stakeholders, which approach to do so are you using?

985. What is the impact on the Business Case?

986. Who are the members of the governing body?

987. Do you prepare stakeholder engagement plans?

988. Are they needed?

989. How do you reply to this question; you am new here and managing this major program. How do you suggest you build your network?

990. Which team member will work with each stakeholder?

991. What steps can you take for positive relationships?

992. Where do team members get information?

993. What is the impact on the risks?

994. What is the status of the issue?

995. Why not more evaluators?

4.0 Monitoring and Controlling Process Group: Improving Performance

996. Purpose: toward what end is the evaluation being conducted?

997. How many more potential communications channels were introduced by the discovery of the new stakeholders?

998. Is the program making progress in helping to achieve the set results?

999. Is it what was agreed upon?

1000. How well did the chosen processes fit the needs of the Improving Performance project?

1001. How well did the team follow the chosen processes?

1002. When will the Improving Performance project be done?

1003. How is agile Improving Performance project management done?

1004. How is agile portfolio management done?

1005. How were collaborations developed, and how are they sustained?

1006. Propriety: who needs to be involved in the evaluation to be ethical?

1007. What is the timeline?

1008. How is Agile Improving Performance project Management done?

1009. Did the Improving Performance project team have the right skills?

1010. What departments are involved in its daily operation?

1011. Measurable - are the targets measurable?

4.1 Project Performance Report: Improving Performance

1012. To what degree do individual skills and abilities match task demands?

1013. To what degree are the skill areas critical to team performance present?

1014. To what degree will team members, individually and collectively, commit time to help themselves and others learn and develop skills?

1015. To what degree does the information network provide individuals with the information they require?

1016. What is the degree to which rules govern information exchange between individuals within your organization?

1017. To what degree are fresh input and perspectives systematically caught and added (for example, through information and analysis, new members, and senior sponsors)?

1018. To what degree does the task meet individual needs?

1019. To what degree are the goals realistic?

1020. How is the data used?

1021. To what degree are the goals ambitious?

1022. To what degree does the teams purpose constitute a broader, deeper aspiration than just accomplishing short-term goals?

1023. To what degree do team members agree with the goals, relative importance, and the ways in which achievement will be measured?

1024. To what degree are the members clear on what they are individually responsible for and what they are jointly responsible for?

1025. To what degree does the team possess adequate membership to achieve its ends?

1026. To what degree do team members frequently explore the teams purpose and its implications?

4.2 Variance Analysis: Improving Performance

1027. Who are responsible for the establishment of budgets and assignment of resources for overhead performance?

1028. Contemplated overhead expenditure for each period based on the best information currently is available?

1029. What types of services and expense are shared between business segments?

1030. Budget versus actual. how does the monthly budget compare to actual experience?

1031. What business event caused the fluctuation?

1032. Are overhead cost budgets established for each department which has authority to incur overhead costs?

1033. What causes selling price variance?

1034. Are records maintained to show how management reserves are used?

1035. Does the contractors system provide unit or lot costs when applicable?

1036. Is the anticipated (firm and potential) business base Improving Performance projected in a rational, consistent manner?

1037. How do you evaluate the impact of schedule changes, work around, et?

1038. Are estimates of costs at completion generated in a rational, consistent manner?

1039. What does a favorable labor efficiency variance mean?

1040. Historical experience?

1041. Is the market likely to continue to grow at this rate next year?

1042. Does the contractors system include procedures for measuring the performance of critical subcontractors?

1043. Are the actual costs used for variance analysis reconcilable with data from the accounting system?

1044. Are all cwbs elements specified for external reporting?

4.3 Earned Value Status: Improving Performance

1045. How does this compare with other Improving Performance projects?

1046. Where is evidence-based earned value in your organization reported?

1047. When is it going to finish?

1048. Earned value can be used in almost any Improving Performance project situation and in almost any Improving Performance project environment. it may be used on large Improving Performance projects, medium sized Improving Performance projects, tiny Improving Performance projects (in cut-down form), complex and simple Improving Performance projects and in any market sector. some people, of course, know all about earned value, they have used it for years - but perhaps not as effectively as they could have?

1049. What is the unit of forecast value?

1050. How much is it going to cost by the finish?

1051. Where are your problem areas?

1052. Validation is a process of ensuring that the developed system will actually achieve the stakeholders desired outcomes; Are you building the right product? What do you validate?

1053. Are you hitting your Improving Performance projects targets?

1054. If earned value management (EVM) is so good in determining the true status of a Improving Performance project and Improving Performance project its completion, why is it that hardly any one uses it in information systems related Improving Performance projects?

1055. Verification is a process of ensuring that the developed system satisfies the stakeholders agreements and specifications; Are you building the product right? What do you verify?

4.4 Risk Audit: Improving Performance

1056. Who is responsible for what?

1057. Have all possible risks/hazards been identified (including injury to staff, damage to equipment, impact on others in the community)?

1058. Do your financial policies and procedures ensure that each step in financial handling (receipt, recording, banking, reporting) is not completed by one person?

1059. What is the effect of globalisation; is business becoming too complex and can the auditor rely on auditing standards?

1060. How do you compare to other jurisdictions when managing the risk of ....?

1061. Number of users of the product?

1062. Have top software and customer managers formally committed to support the Improving Performance project?

1063. Are Improving Performance project requirements stable?

1064. Do you have position descriptions for all key paid and volunteer positions in your organization?

1065. Are corresponding safety and risk management policies posted for all to see?

1066. Does your auditor understand your business?

1067. What impact does prior experience have on decisions made during the risk-assessment process?

1068. Will participants be required to sign a legally counselled waiver or risk disclaimer when entering an event?

1069. Do you have proper induction processes for all new paid staff and volunteers who have a specific role and responsibility?

1070. What are the Internal Controls ?

1071. What does internal control mean in the context of the audit process?

1072. Do you meet the legislative requirements (for example PAYG, super contributions) for paid employees?

1073. Are end-users enthusiastically committed to the Improving Performance project and the system/product to be built?

1074. To what extent should analytical procedures be utilized in the risk-assessment process?

1075. Tradeoff: how much risk can be tolerated and still deliver the products where they need to be?

4.5 Contractor Status Report: Improving Performance

1076. What was the budget or estimated cost for your organizations services?

1077. If applicable; describe your standard schedule for new software version releases. Are new software version releases included in the standard maintenance plan?

1078. What are the minimum and optimal bandwidth requirements for the proposed solution?

1079. How long have you been using the services?

1080. What is the average response time for answering a support call?

1081. How is risk transferred?

1082. Are there contractual transfer concerns?

1083. What was the actual budget or estimated cost for your organizations services?

1084. What was the overall budget or estimated cost?

1085. Describe how often regular updates are made to the proposed solution. Are corresponding regular updates included in the standard maintenance plan?

1086. Who can list a Improving Performance project

as organization experience, your organization or a previous employee of your organization?

1087. How does the proposed individual meet each requirement?

1088. What process manages the contracts?

1089. What was the final actual cost?

4.6 Formal Acceptance: Improving Performance

1090. Was the client satisfied with the Improving Performance project results?

1091. Did the Improving Performance project achieve its MOV?

1092. General estimate of the costs and times to complete the Improving Performance project?

1093. Was the Improving Performance project managed well?

1094. Was the sponsor/customer satisfied?

1095. Do you perform formal acceptance or burn-in tests?

1096. What features, practices, and processes proved to be strengths or weaknesses?

1097. Did the Improving Performance project manager and team act in a professional and ethical manner?

1098. How well did the team follow the methodology?

1099. Have all comments been addressed?

1100. Who would use it?

1101. What was done right?

1102. How does your team plan to obtain formal acceptance on your Improving Performance project?

1103. Was the Improving Performance project work done on time, within budget, and according to specification?

1104. Who supplies data?

1105. Was business value realized?

1106. What is the Acceptance Management Process?

1107. Do you buy pre-configured systems or build your own configuration?

1108. What are the requirements against which to test, Who will execute?

1109. Was the Improving Performance project goal achieved?

5.0 Closing Process Group: Improving Performance

1110. How well defined and documented were the Improving Performance project management processes you chose to use?

1111. What was learned?

1112. What areas were overlooked on this Improving Performance project?

1113. Was the schedule met?

1114. What is the Improving Performance project Management Process?

1115. How well did the chosen processes produce the expected results?

1116. What is the overall risk of the Improving Performance project to your organization?

1117. How critical is the Improving Performance project success to the success of your organization?

1118. Were the outcomes different from the already stated planned?

1119. What could be done to improve the process?

1120. Are there funding or time constraints?

1121. Were decisions made in a timely manner?

1122. Were cost budgets met?

1123. What were the actual outcomes?

1124. What is the risk of failure to your organization?

1125. Who are the Improving Performance project stakeholders?

1126. What could have been improved?

1127. What areas were overlooked on this Improving Performance project?

1128. What is an Encumbrance?

5.1 Procurement Audit: Improving Performance

1129. Are procurement policies and practices in line with (international) good practice standards?

1130. Is the procurement Improving Performance project efficiently managed?

1131. Are there policies regarding special approval for capital expenditures?

1132. Are there performance targets on value for money obtained and cost savings?

1133. Are there systems for recording and managing stocks (where part of contract)?

1134. Are employees with cash disbursement responsibilities required to take scheduled vacations?

1135. Could the bidders assess the economic risks the successful bidder would be responsible for, thus limiting the inclusion of extra charges for risk?

1136. Does the strategy ensure that appropriate controls are in place to ensure propriety and regularity in delivery?

1137. Were results of the award procedures published?

1138. Are vendor price lists regularly updated?

1139. Is a log maintained over the use of signature plates?

1140. Access to data, including standing data, and the identification of restriction levels and authorised personnel was in place?

1141. Are budget transfers within the general fund made for only the already stated items permitted by law and regulation?

1142. Is there a general policy on approval of purchases?

1143. Have guidelines incorporating the principles and objectives of a robust procurement practice been established?

1144. Have guidelines been set up for how the procurement process should be conducted?

1145. Are there procedures governing the negotiations of long-term contracts?

1146. Were any additional works or deliveries admissible, without recourse to a new procurement procedure?

1147. Has an upper limit of cost been fixed?

1148. Are signature plates under the control of someone other than the individual given check-signing accountability?

5.2 Contract Close-Out: Improving Performance

1149. Change in knowledge?

1150. Change in attitude or behavior?

1151. Parties: Authorized?

1152. How is the contracting office notified of the automatic contract close-out?

1153. Have all acceptance criteria been met prior to final payment to contractors?

1154. Have all contract records been included in the Improving Performance project archives?

1155. Was the contract complete without requiring numerous changes and revisions?

1156. What is capture management?

1157. Why Outsource?

1158. Have all contracts been closed?

1159. Change in circumstances?

1160. Was the contract type appropriate?

1161. Have all contracts been completed?

1162. Are the signers the authorized officials?

1163. Parties: who is involved?

1164. How does it work?

1165. What happens to the recipient of services?

1166. How/when used ?

1167. Has each contract been audited to verify acceptance and delivery?

1168. Was the contract sufficiently clear so as not to result in numerous disputes and misunderstandings?

5.3 Project or Phase Close-Out: Improving Performance

1169. What is this stakeholder expecting?

1170. What stakeholder group needs, expectations, and interests are being met by the Improving Performance project?

1171. Have business partners been involved extensively, and what data was required for them?

1172. In preparing the Lessons Learned report, should it reflect a consensus viewpoint, or should the report reflect the different individual viewpoints?

1173. Did the Improving Performance project management methodology work?

1174. Which changes might a stakeholder be required to make as a result of the Improving Performance project?

1175. If you were the Improving Performance project sponsor, how would you determine which Improving Performance project team(s) and/or individuals deserve recognition?

1176. What can you do better next time, and what specific actions can you take to improve?

1177. Is the lesson based on actual Improving Performance project experience rather than on independent research?

1178. Who are the Improving Performance project stakeholders and what are roles and involvement?

1179. Did the delivered product meet the specified requirements and goals of the Improving Performance project?

1180. Complete yes or no?

1181. Who exerted influence that has positively affected or negatively impacted the Improving Performance project?

1182. How much influence did the stakeholder have over others?

1183. What benefits or impacts does the stakeholder group expect to obtain as a result of the Improving Performance project?

5.4 Lessons Learned: Improving Performance

1184. What did you do right?

1185. What things surprised you on the Improving Performance project that were not in the plan?

1186. How to write up the lesson identified – how will you document the results of your analysis corresponding that you have an li ready to take the next step in the ll process?

1187. What things mattered the most on this Improving Performance project?

1188. Would you spend your own money to fix this issue?

1189. What are the performance measures?

1190. What is your working hypothesis, if you have one?

1191. How efficient were Improving Performance project team meetings conducted?

1192. What is your organizational ideology?

1193. How effectively and timely was your organizational change impact identified and planned for?

1194. What is (are) the indicator(s) of success?

1195. How effective was the acceptance management process?

1196. Were any objectives unmet?

1197. What if anything has been lacking?

1198. How many interest groups are stakeholders?

1199. Was the necessary hardware, software, accommodation etc available?

1200. Under what legal authority did your organization head and program manager direct your organization and Improving Performance project?

1201. What worked well or did not work well, either for this Improving Performance project or for the Improving Performance project team?

1202. What were the main sources of frustration in the Improving Performance project?

1203. What would you like to see better documented about how to use existing processes on this type of Improving Performance project?

Index

effects 48, 131, 135-136, 163
efficiency   54, 62, 103, 227, 245
efficient   54, 85, 219, 262
effort 35, 53, 57, 107, 156, 196, 236
efforts 34, 88, 191
either 161, 235, 263
electronic   1
element   156, 158
elements   11-12, 31, 66, 103, 115, 155, 190-191, 230, 236, 245
elicit 190
eliminated   191
e-mail 146
embarking   38
emerging   67, 95
emphasis   225
employed   196
employee   83, 113, 237, 251
employees   25-27, 63, 109, 124, 237, 249, 256
employers   134
empower   7
enable 70
enablers   125
encourage   82, 98
endure 180
end-users   249
engage   123, 197, 234, 236
engagement 45, 134, 238
enhance   94, 171
enhanced   123
enhancing   93
enough   7, 63, 110, 112, 114, 147, 203
ensure 28, 37, 60, 68, 107, 112, 117, 119-120, 135, 172, 180, 186, 189, 195, 248, 256
ensures   112
ensuring   10, 123, 137, 246-247
entail 56
entails 227
entering   249
Enterprise   219
entities 53
entitled   212
entity 1

provided   8, 13, 92, 158, 171, 177, 211, 229
providers   89
provides   146, 228
providing   99, 134, 175, 228
provision   213
published   256
publisher   1
pulled 110
purchase   9, 11
purchased   11
purchases   257
purpose   2, 11, 105, 132, 149, 181, 190, 222, 235, 240, 243
purposes   178
pushing   114
qualified   30, 63, 65, 68, 140, 142, 158
qualifies   59, 61
qualify 58, 64
qualities   20
quality 1, 4-5, 11, 26, 48, 53, 60, 64, 68, 73, 89, 93, 95, 118, 157-
158, 183, 185, 187-190, 193-195, 209, 217, 221, 226-228
quantified   102
quantify   58
quantities   212
question   12-13, 17, 28, 44, 59, 76, 92, 105, 111, 190, 238
questions   7, 9, 12, 62, 173
quickly 12, 60, 64, 73
radically   71
raised 149
Ranged   178
rather 111, 260
rating 211, 222, 236
ratings 211
rational   155, 244-245
rationale   210, 226
reached   24
reaching   126
reactivate   106
readable   212
reader 141
readings   93
realistic   24, 68, 107, 140, 157, 176, 217, 242
reality 183
realize 46

sanitized   151
satisfied   111, 143, 252
satisfies 247
satisfying   123
savings 36, 46, 55, 74, 256
scalable   78
scenario   30, 36, 217
schedule   3-4, 38, 46, 97, 124, 137, 145, 155, 157, 165, 170-
171, 175-178, 183-184, 192, 200, 209-210, 223, 230, 245, 250, 254
scheduled   141, 143, 177, 179, 211, 256
schedules   165, 176, 192, 212
scheduling   213
scheme   98
science   66
scopes 150
Scorecard   2, 13-15
scorecards   96
Scores 15
scoring 11
Screen 221
screening   187
seamless   124
second   13
Seconds   232
section 13, 27, 43, 58, 74, 91, 104, 127-128
sections   214
sector 246
securing   45, 113
security   20, 66, 83, 94, 98, 134, 151, 188, 223
segmented   42
segments   37, 115, 244
select 61, 101
selected   86, 181-182
selection   5, 170, 211, 218, 235
seller   170
sellers   1
selling 126, 163, 244
senior   87, 99, 107, 123, 242
sensitive   41
separated   156
sequence   172
sequencing   122, 196
series   12